"We really enjoyed reading this book and were pleased about two things in particular. The content of the book is informative and is so in plain, understandable, and non-challenging language; and Priscilla and Aquila are shown to be warm, admirable, and true-to-life people, not implausible artificial types. Noël Keller has made them a couple with whom it would be a delight to share hospitality, a privilege to have available for guidance, and a blessing to be ceaselessly certain of their friendship and love."

—Ed and Mary Flood
Married Lay Ministers
Wheaton, Maryland

"If anyone still thinks that history is boring, they should read Marie Noël Keller's book. By drawing out the historical implications of clues found in six short passages, she has reconstructed the history within which Priscilla and Aquila lived and enabled that couple to come alive. Though she reinforces her careful exegetical work with the insights of other scholars in the field, she has produced a work that even the non-scholarly will find imminently readable. By the end of the book, Pricilla and Aquila have become people you want to know and model your life after."

—Dianne Bergant
Author of *Scripture: History and
Interpretation* (Liturgical Press)

"While teaching Paul over a twenty-year span I often called attention to the importance of Paul's missionary co-workers, Priscilla and Aquila, but with little follow up. Noël Keller offers a superb close reading of all New Testament references, making this couple come alive, while offering great insights into Early Christian communities. Carefully researched, with ample bibliography and evocative suggestions about how their lives challenge the church today, this book should be a *vade mecum* for anyone interested in Pauline Christianity."

—John R. Donahue, SJ
`esearch Professor in Theology
.oyola University Maryland

D1562524

"Dr. Keller has achieved a perfect example of that rare book which is both rigorously scholarly and completely readable. Without polemic, she illuminates Priscilla's prominence in this ministerial couple whom Paul commended as fellow workers and upon whom he depended. She leads the reader through the Priscilla and Aquila material in the New Testament, filling in the context in ways that make their ministry and house churches come alive and their relevance for contemporary church practice clear.

"Highly recommended reading for anyone interested in early Christianity, the history of missions, the authority and ministry of women in the church and paradigms for new forms of mutual ministry."

—Bonnie B. Thurston, PhD
Author of *The Spiritual Landscape of Mark* (Liturgical Press)

"Noël Keller produces a surprising, fascinating interpretation of Priscilla and Aquila as missionaries for Christ, 'advance workers' for Paul in Corinth, Ephesus, and Rome, playing a unique role among Paul's social network. The household was the primary setting for their activity, combining as it did work space, retail shop, and living quarters, interpreting this from the social world of the Eastern Roman empire. They prepared for and enabled Paul's evangelistic activity in these major urban centers of the Greek east, thus making clear that Paul was not a loner, but the center of a lively group of people who supported and enabled his missionary activity. Active long before there was an 'ordained clergy' in the Christian community, Priscilla and Aquila model how ordinary Christians impact mightily the proclamation of Jesus Christ."

—Edgar Krentz
Christ Seminary–Seminex Professor of New Testament, Emeritus Lutheran School of Theology, Chicago

Paul's Social Network: Brothers and Sisters in Faith
Bruce J. Malina, Series Editor

Priscilla and Aquila

Paul's Coworkers in Christ Jesus

Marie Noël Keller

A Michael Glazier Book

LITURGICAL PRESS
Collegeville, Minnesota

www.litpress.org

A Michael Glazier Book published by Liturgical Press

Cover design by Ann Blattner. *Saint Paul*, fresco fragment, Roma, 13th century.

Photo credits: page 17, Liturgical Press Archives; page 21, David Manahan, OSB; page 59, iStockphoto, © Bojan Pavlukovic.

1   2   3   4   5   6   7   8   9

Library of Congress Cataloging-in-Publication Data

Keller, Marie Noël.
    Priscilla and Aquila : Paul's coworkers in Christ Jesus / Marie Noël Keller.
        p.   cm.—(Paul's Social Network: Brothers and Sisters in Faith)
    "A Michael Glazier book."
    Includes bibliographical references (p.   ) and indexes.
    ISBN 978-0-8146-5284-8 — ISBN 978-0-8146-8001-8 (e-book)
    1. Paul, the Apostle, Saint—Friends and associates.   2. Priscilla, Saint, 1st cent.   3. Aquila, Saint, 1st cent.   I. Title.

BS2506.3.K45   2010
226.6092'2—dc22   2010017281

In gratitude for mercies given and received

CONTENTS

PREFACE

Human beings are embedded in a set of social relations. A social network is one way of conceiving that set of social relations in terms of a number of persons connected to one another by varying degrees of relatedness. In the early Jesus group documents featuring Paul and coworkers, it takes little effort to envision the apostle's collection of friends and friends of friends that is the Pauline network.

This set of brief books consists of a description of some of the significant persons who constituted the Pauline network. For Christians of the Western tradition, these persons are significant ancestors in faith. While each of them is worth knowing by themselves, it is largely because of their standing within that web of social relations woven about and around Paul that they are of lasting interest. Through this series we hope to come to know those persons in ways befitting their first-century Mediterranean culture.

Bruce J. Malina
Creighton University
Series Editor

ACKNOWLEDGMENTS

I f there is one thing I have learned in my studies over the years, it is this: text without context is pretext. Accordingly, three aspects of my life give flesh to the words I have written:

- the privilege of shepherding an Institute on Sacred Scripture at Misericordia University, Dallas, Pennsylvania, for over thirty years. Besides hearing wonderful presentations, it has afforded me the opportunity of seeing firsthand the incredible hunger people have for the Word of God and the extent to which they will sacrifice to hear it.

- the privilege of shepherding our Mercy Associate program. Through it and my travels throughout the United States giving talks and retreats I have been continually inspired by countless women and men from all walks of life who have partnered with Catherine McAuley, the foundress of the Sisters of Mercy, and who daily embody her vision in the same ways Priscilla and Aquila lived out their own commitment.

- friends and teachers who have encouraged, challenged, and supported me and from whose lived reality of the words I learn/learned: Julia L. Ford; Brother Luke Salm, FSC; Edgar Krentz; Bruce Malina; and Sister Cor Mariae Mulhern, RSM, are a few examples. Most recently, I wish to thank Mary Theresa Glynn, RSM, and Lauren L. Murphy who painstakingly plowed through my text and who taught me the meaning of "every jot and tittle."

You are a presence that strengthens.

INTRODUCTION:
A PRESENCE TO STRENGTHEN

During a trip to Innsbruck, Austria, I visited the Cathedral of St. James where I learned from the docent that in the past statues were placed on the facades of churches as a reminder to their parishioners that the saints they represented would stand guard outside to protect them.[1] Indeed, it was thought one proceeded from the chaos of the outer world (west, back door of the church) toward the light of the eastern part of the church, where the Blessed Sacrament and altar were situated. Similarly, Eastern Christians revered and still revere icons, since they believed and yet believe an image can make a holy person a real presence in their home or church and that a faithful representation of an icon achieves this. Western Christians use pictures and illustrations that they hang on their walls, use as bookmarks, or carry in their wallets. Such practices are in the hope that the reminder of the person or persons depicted on them (whether alive or dead) will strengthen, protect, and inspire them.

The ancients used their own or other people's example as concrete models in their rhetoric to imitate or learn from. Positive examples were employed to show listeners how they were to act while negative examples illustrated behaviors people were to avoid. Plutarch, for example, wrote his *Lives* in part to provide his readers with models for conduct. The advice Seneca offers his friend Lucilius (*Ep.* 11:8-10) epitomizes with what importance the use of example was held in the ancient world:

Hear and take to heart this useful and wholesome motto: "Cherish some man of high character, and keep him ever before your eyes, living as if he were watching you, and ordering all your actions as if he beheld them." Such my dear Lucilius, is the counsel of Epicurus; he has quite properly given us a guardian and an attendant. We can get rid of most sins, if we have a witness who stands near us when we are likely to go wrong. The soul should have someone whom it can respect,—one by whose authority it may make even its inner shrine more hallowed. Happy is the man who can make others better, not merely when he is in their company, but even when he is in their thoughts! And happy also is he who can so revere a man as to calm and regulate himself by calling him to mind! One who can so revere another, will soon be himself worthy of reverence. . . . Choose a master whose life, conversation, and soul-expressing face have satisfied you; picture him always to yourself as your protector or your pattern. For we must indeed have someone according to whom we may regulate our characters; you can never straighten that which is crooked unless you use a ruler.[2]

Paul uses examples in his letters (Jesus, Timothy, Epaphroditus, and himself in Philippians, etc.), as Luke does in his gospel and Acts (e.g., Acts 4:36–5:11). This book is concerned with one of Luke's examples, that of Priscilla and Aquila, a couple who are associated with Paul. They are the second couple in Acts to be given significant narrative development. The first, Ananias and Sapphira are a negative example (Acts 5:1-11), while this artisan duo, who are in more scenes than many other second-tiered people in the New Testament, are an extremely positive one.

Priscilla and Aquila make six appearances in the New Testament and their importance is highlighted by three different authors. Twice they are mentioned in Paul (1 Cor 16:19; Rom 16:3); three times by Luke in Acts (18:1-3, 18-19, 26-27); and once in a Deutero-Pauline letter (2 Tim 4:19). Later, John Chrysostom (347–407 CE) comments on them in several of his homilies (Homily 40 on the Acts of the Apostles [18:18], Homily 44 on

First Corinthians [see 16:19], Homily 30 on Romans [16:3-5], and Homily 10 on Second Timothy [4:9-13]). And he elaborates on them in his First Homily on the Greeting to Priscilla and Aquila (Rom 16:3-4) which is also known as "Salutate Priscillam et Aquilam. Most recently, they were the focus of one of Pope Benedict XVI's reflections (cf. General Audience, February 7, 2007). Today churches celebrate Sts. Priscilla and Aquila, evidencing that Luke's nomenclature was adopted.[3] Indeed, Luke refers to Paul's Prisca, her more formal name, by its affectionate diminutive Priscilla, as he does in his references to Silvanus (Silas) and Sosipatros (Sopatros).[4] Unless I am quoting Paul, I will use the name Priscilla.

Nomenclature and Status

Priscilla and Aquila have good Roman names in a Graecized form. *Priskilla* is a form of the feminine Latin adjective *prisca*, which means "primitive or ancient," while *Akylas* is a form of the Latin cognomen (nickname) *Aquila*, which means "eagle." As it was quite common for Judean, Greek, or Latin-speaking people to have Roman names in Rome,[5] this custom was probably also held in the Roman provinces. Such would be the case in Pontus, which is the birthplace of Aquila. Most Judeans of the Diaspora, however they adapted themselves to their surroundings, were Greek-speaking, and their names would be Graecized.[6]

Much ink has been spent on the placement of Priscilla and Aquila's names in the texts; for in four of the six places in which their names occur (Rom 16:3; Acts 18:18, 26; 2 Tim 4:19) Priscilla's name comes before her husband's. Such precedence was an unconventional occurrence; in fact, women were hardly mentioned at all. Yet there is no consensus as to why her name appears first. For some scholars, Priscilla's wealth and status gives her precedence, as her name indicates she belonged by birth or manumission to the *gens Acilia*, who were an influential family among the Roman nobility.[7] Jerome Murphy-O'Connor disagrees, for to him, the fact that Priscilla worked manually with her husband (Acts 18:3) indicates she neither outranked Aquila in social class nor had independent wealth. Besides, had she been a woman of noble birth, she would not have known how to do the heavy needle-and-palm work of tentmakers, nor would her hands be adapted to it, since women of independent means did not need to work.[8] And surely, had she had elevated status, Luke would have mentioned it, as he did other distinguished women in his work (Luke 8:3; Acts 16:14; 17:4, 12, 34).

Instead, Murphy-O'Connor and other scholars think the priority of Priscilla's name was achieved by her greater prominence in the life of the church.[9] As Linda L. Belleville avers:

> When New Testament writers refer to their occupation of tentmakers and to "their house," the order is "Aquila and Priscilla" (Acts 18:2; 1 Cor 16:19). But when ministry is in view, the order is "Priscilla and Aquila" (Acts 18:18; Rom 16:3; cf. 2 Tim 4:19). This is also the case with the introduction of Apollos (Acts 18:26), suggesting that Priscilla possessed the dominant ministry and leadership skills of the duo.[10]

To further her claim, Belleville points to Luke's usual way of ordering the names of the ministry teams in Acts, for when the famous missionaries are commissioned by the church in Antioch, the order is "Barnabas and Paul" (Acts 11:30; 12:25; 13:2-7); but when Saul takes the lead, the order becomes "Paul and Barnabas" (Acts 13: 9-12, 43; 14:12, 20; 15:2, 22, 35). Acts 15:12 and 15:25 are two exceptions. Here, political diplomacy and expediency dictate his order.[11] Likewise, in Paul's long list of greetings to and from people in Romans 16, Gaius with his spacious dwelling, and Erastus, the city treasurer, appear last (Rom 16:21-23). As such, it appears Paul esteemed a person's work for the church (Rom 16:3b, 4, 5a, 21) more than their status in the wider society (Gal 3:28).

Whatever the case, whether Priscilla's primacy is the result of her status, or her place in the church—as John Chrysostom, hardly an affirmer of women, recognizes (cf. Homily 10 on Second Timothy [v. 19, see pp. 54–55] or First Homily on the Greeting to Priscilla and Aquila [Rom 16:3-4, see p. 25])—or, for that matter, the result of both reasons,[12] for today's church, F. Scott Spencer's insight cannot be lost. He maintains the alternating order of their names simply reinforces the mutuality of this couple's relationship. They are interchangeable collegial partners,[13] which is exactly what Meinrad Craighead's illustration of Priscilla and Aquila depicts.[14]

Priscilla and Aquila are a positive example of a team ministry, to the point that both in Luke and Paul, except for Luke's notice of Aquila's beginnings, they are never mentioned apart from one another! Moreover, their prominence in and among the nascent Jesus groups is evidenced by the fact they are the first persons Paul lists in his long set of greetings in Romans 16.

Journeying Forth

It is often argued that all of Acts is Luke's literary composition and that the sequences within his work merely serve to promote his agenda. I think this is so. But what is his agenda? Perhaps, we need to remember that Luke, and the other evangelists, are essentially "pastors." As such, I imagine each of them coming to the table on which all of the material that was known about Jesus and his early followers could be found, that is, parables, stories, sayings, vignettes, etc., and taking from it those pieces that would be most helpful to the life and needs of their respective communities. Because of the single-mindedness of their focus, none of them had any compunction about changing the details, for they were just making sure that what they were proclaiming was clearly understood. A serious look at any page of "Gospel Parallels" affirms this assertion.

In Luke's case, the first four sentences of his gospel, which are really one sentence (Luke 1:1-4), also function as an introduction to his second volume, Acts (1:1). Moreover, they tell us what he is about. Clearly, he announces that his work(s) will give the people for whom he writes "assurance," because through them, he will demonstrate the reliability of "the things of which they have been informed." In fact, Luke underscores this point by putting the Greek term *asphaleia* (reliability/assurance) at the end of his sentence. It is in the emphatic position! Thereafter, whatever he chooses to report in either volume has importance, which includes the things he will assert about Priscilla and Aquila. Indeed, each sequence in Luke-Acts is a narrative depiction of how God works and continues to work through Jesus and those who follow him.

I too want to approach the texts regarding Priscilla and Aquila, Paul's coworkers in Christ Jesus, in the same manner Luke did. In some instances Luke's details can be cross-referenced, while in others, he will give us singular information. In either case, the combined material will help us to see the big picture. It will also bring us to the point of learning. For this reason, I will use the canonical text as my reference and when necessary, point out the variants, i.e., the additions and deletions that are available.[15]

As we embark on this study, let us use Craighead's illustration of Priscilla and Aquila to call them into our personal space, to strengthen and inspire us.[16] Let us also ask the right question.

The question is not, "Is every element of their story true?" But rather, "What does God want us to learn from their story?" Finally, let us employ the methodology known as "passing over and coming back." Here, one "passes over" from their own life or standpoint to that of another or others' lives and, through dialogue, enters into a sympathetic understanding of their life or standpoint. Then, finding resonances, or perhaps even a challenge, between themselves and the other, one "comes back" once again to one's own life having learned something.[17] It is a dangerous adventure and not for the faint of heart, since you could be changed!

Before We Start:
A Word about Anachronistic Language

It is important to recognize that during the Second Temple and New Testament periods, the words "Jew" (*Ioudaios*) and "Judaism" (*Ioudaismos*) did not mean what contemporary society means by them. For today, these terms refer to the liturgy and customs, etc., of the Jewish religion that were made normative by the Babylonian Talmud in the fifth to sixth century CE and to the people who practice them. In the time of Jesus, however, Greek words ending in *-aios* meant "of or pertaining to the place named." As such, people of the Mediterranean called all members of the house of Israel "Judeans" after the region in which the temple, the central place of worship was located—Jerusalem in Judea.[18] Concomitantly, *Ioudaismos* described the behavior of Judeans or the people in Judea.

The term "Christian," as it is used today, did not exist in Jesus' time either, despite the modern translation of Acts 11:26. Instead, in using the term *Christianos*, peoples of the Mediterranean would be referring to those persons who belonged to the political faction of *Christos* (Messiah) and who they considered were members of the Messianist party. Today, "Christian" refers to anyone who embraces the religion that was formalized through the doctrines of the Councils of Nicea (325 CE) and Chalcedon

(451 CE). Men and women who proclaimed Jesus as the Messiah of God in both Luke's and Paul's time, however, would never have thought of themselves as *Christianos* in either of the senses that have already been listed. Instead, they saw themselves as "Jesus followers" or "Christ believers," and they would have referred to themselves, or talked about other early believers as members of a specific Jesus group such as the one at Corinth. We will use "Jew" and "Christian" in the same way the early believers used these terms throughout this study.

CHAPTER 1

Luke's Narration
(Acts 18:1-3, 18-19, 26-27)

Luke introduces Priscilla and Aquila in the second half of his narrative, which he devotes to the achievements of Paul. Accordingly, they are, as any other person Luke identifies, "supporting players" to his hero and star. That this couple appear at all, in spite of his focus, accentuates their importance and the enormous influence they had on many people in those early years. We meet them here in the context of Paul's second missionary journey and, at first, within the framework of his mission to Corinth. Indeed, they will appear three times in chapter 18. We will examine each scene to see how Priscilla and Aquila interface with Paul and then suggest how they impacted the lives and faith of the early believers.

Interfacing with Paul

Scene One: Acts 18:1-3

After this [Paul] left Athens and went to Corinth. And he found a [Judean] named Aquila, a native of Pontus, lately come from Italy with his wife Priscilla, because Claudius had commanded all the [Judeans] to leave Rome. And he went to see them; and because he was of the same trade he stayed with them, and they worked, for by trade they were tentmakers.

Context

Paul has just left Athens where his message about Jesus received a mixed hearing from the Athenians (see p. 16). From there he traveled a little more than forty miles west to the Roman colony of Corinth, which was an important port city located at the principal juncture in the best sea route between Rome and Italy in the west and what is now called Greece and other areas to the east. Its position on a narrow four- and one-half mile isthmus enabled ships to transfer their cargoes by way of a paved road (*diolkos*) that connected both the Corinthian and Saronic Gulfs. In so doing, the dangerous 187-mile, six-day trip around the rocky southern tip of the Peloponnese was no longer necessary. For such reasons, Corinth became the most important trade route between the eastern and western parts of the empire. All traffic, land or sea, east-, west-, north- or southbound, passed through it.

Besides tradespeople, Corinth attracted visitors for other reasons. Pilgrims came for healing at the city's Asclepeion and drama enthusiasts, to enjoy plays, music, and oratory in its large theater. Likewise, it was a stone's throw from the site of the Isthmian Games, which were a biennial spring celebration of Poseidon and the second most important competition of the four great Panhellenic festivals. Indeed, as Corinth was a city bustling with life, it attracted people of all kinds, particularly those interested in being part of "a new thing." Accordingly, it was the type of place Paul's strategic eye discerned as a promising center for making contacts with all sorts of people. As such, it was an ideal site to spread the message about Jesus. With so many transients, it was also a space where he could earn a living.

The emperor Claudius restored Achaia as a senatorial province in 44 CE with its capital at Corinth. Thereafter

the Senate was represented by an annually appointed proconsul (governor). An inscription mentioning Gallio as
proconsul from July 51 to June 52 is virtually the only
ascertainable basis for a chronology of Paul's mission in
general (see Acts 18:12-16). Reckoning with this date, most
scholars have concluded that the eighteen months Paul
spent in Corinth ran from the beginning of 50 to the early
summer of 51.[1]

Most likely, the first thing Paul did when he arrived in Corinth
was to find the location of the synagogue (Acts 18:5, 14; cf. 14:1;
16:3; etc.). Paul never mentions this detail, but his zeal for God
lets us know Luke's notice is more than a possibility. Here,
among other things, he could locate the section where the guild
of "tentmakers" sat. It is also here that *he found a [Judean] named
Aquila*" (Acts 18:2; emphasis added) and, to be sure, Priscilla
with him (cf. Acts 18:26).

First Things

Luke tells us four things about Aquila and Priscilla when he
introduces them in Acts 18:2. They are (1) a married couple (2)
recently expelled from Rome (3) who relocate in Corinth as tentmakers and/or leatherworkers and (4) with whom Paul lives
and works. By examining each piece, we will discover there is
more in these statements than is first evident.

(1) Aquila and Priscilla Are a Married Couple

Luke conveys two formative things about Aquila: he is a
Judean (*ioudaios*) and he hails from Pontus; i.e., he is a "man of
Pontus" by race/nation, which means he was originally a Diaspora Judean.[2] How he got to Rome is a matter of speculation.
Scholarly possibilities range from Aquila being an independent
businessman-adventurer looking for greener pastures[3] to his
being a free man, slave, or freed slave of the Roman Acilian
family, within whose house he met Priscilla, who was herself a

free woman, slave, or daughter of a freedman of the same family.[4] Most recently, Peter Lampe presents a new and intriguing possibility; for in using epigraphical material, he shows that both Priscilla's and Aquila's names were not slave names and thereby asserts that they must have been born free persons.[5] No matter how they started their lives though, by the time we meet them, most interpreters think they are already married.

Some scholars caution against immediately jumping to this conclusion, arguing that since Luke alone explicitly identifies this couple as married, it may be his way of demonstrating the respectability of the Jesus believers.[6] Furthermore, as legal marriages were only possible between free people in the Roman Empire, slaves and freed persons had no guarantee they could enjoy stable relationships. Therefore, as nascent Jesus believers came from the various strata, there had to be an alternative way of understanding missionary pairing. "Spiritual Marriage," that is, couples living together without a physical union, provided a solution whereby people who were unable to be married legally could be together on mission.[7] Scholars who hold this position, then, point to the question Paul asks in 1 Corinthians 9:5, which they translate "Do we not have the right *to have a sister with us as a wife*?" in a "spiritual marriage" sense.[8] Let us attend to their two objections.

First, there is no reason why Paul would have to state "Prisca" and Aquila are married, as in the instances he mentions them (1 Cor 16:19; Rom 16:3), the communities to whom Paul writes and to whom they send their greetings already knew they were. Luke's audience, on the other hand, may not have known this detail, which is why he mentions it. Indeed, Paul never asserts that any of the pairs in Romans 16 are married, as Wayne A. Meeks contends they all are.[9] Perhaps some of them had immigrated to Corinth with Priscilla and Aquila and Paul knew them, but he may never have met some of the others on the list. Instead, Priscilla and Aquila probably told him about them. Moreover, Luke uses the term *gynē* as "wife" in the Ananias/ Sapphira narrative: "Ananias with his wife [*gynaiki*] Sapphira" (5:1); "and with his wife's knowledge" (*gynaikos*; 5:2); "After an interval of about three hours his wife [*gynē*] came in" (5:7). Clearly, Luke depicts this couple as anything but respectable. So to say he uses the term merely to demonstrate the respectability of Jesus believers dies on the vine. Married is married!

Second, let us examine Paul's use of *gynē* in 1 Corinthians 9:5. At the outset, the question (really, example) Paul asks (gives) must be seen in its larger context. It is part of an answer to one of the questions the community asked him and that he begins answering in chapter 7. Here he addresses the issue of buying and eating meat previously offered to idols (8:1–11:1) since some members in the community believe they can partake of the meat and in the banquets within which it is served while others do not. In response, while Paul recognizes one's freedom to buy and eat the meat (1 Cor 8:9), he grounds this or any choice a Corinthian believer makes within the framework of what is best for everyone involved (1 Cor 8:10-12). He will repeat this advice later in his letter: "'All things are lawful,' but not all things are helpful. 'All things are lawful,' but not all things build up. Let no one seek his[/her] own good, but the good of his[/her] neighbor" (1 Cor 10:23f.). Then, as any good teacher, Paul gives his own example (1 Cor 8:13), which was a common device used by ancient authors. More persuasive than mere words, it provided a concrete example to imitate. As Seneca advises Lucilius in *Ep* 6:5-6:

> . . . the living voice and the intimacy of a common life will help you more than the written word. You must go to the scene of action, first, because men put more faith in their eyes than in their ears, and second, because the way is long if one follows precepts, but short and helpful, if one follows patterns. Cleanthes could not have been the express image of Zeno, if he had merely heard his lectures; he shared in his life, saw into his hidden purposes, and watched him to see whether he lived according to his own rules.[10]

First Corinthians 9:1-27 is another illustration of Paul's giving up his rights and freedom for the benefit of others. Having a "wife" alongside him as a partner is one of his examples (1 Cor 9:5).[11]

Earlier in his letter Paul uses the term *gynē* as "wife" or "woman." In the instances he uses *gynē*, the term stands alone. For example: "It is well for a man not to touch a woman [*gynaikos*]" (1 Cor 7:1); "each man should have his own wife [*gynaika*]" (7:2); "the wife [*gynaika*] should not separate from her husband" (7:10); "Are you bound to a wife? [*gynaikos*] . . . Are you free from a wife [*gynaika*]?" (7:27); or "Let those who have wives [*gynaikas*] live as though they had none" (7:29). When *gynē* appears again in 1 Corinthians 9:5, however, it is partnered with *adelphēn* (*adelphēn gynaika*), which is a word that means "sister" and that Hans Conzelmann, as others, translates as "Have we not the right to have a sister with us as a wife" in the spiritual marriage sense. Yet Conzelmann also notes that "sister" can mean she is a "believer."[12] Indeed, the references he cites from Paul—1 Corinthians 7:15 (concerning mixed marriages); Romans 16:1 (concerning Phoebe); and Philemon 2 (concerning Apphia)—all imply variant uses of the translation "sister" as either "believer" or "co-missionary." Moreover, earlier in his work, Conzelmann translates 1 Corinthians 7:15 as, "But if the unbelieving partner is for separating, then let him [or her] separate. In such cases the brother or *the sister* is not bound,"[13] which, according to context, I read as "But if the unbelieving partner [in the marriage] is for separating, let him [or her] separate. In such case [the one who is] the believer is not bound." Here "sister" clearly means a believing wife, which is how scholars such as Gordon Fee, Richard Horsley, and Marion Soards translate *adelphēn gynaika* in 1 Corinthians 9:5.[14]

One further piece needs to be examined and that is Paul's use of *adelphos* (brother) and *adelphē* (sister) in other texts. He calls Sosthenes (1 Cor 1:1), Apollos (1 Cor 16:12), Timothy (Phlm 1), Quartus (Rom 16:23), and Epaphroditus (Phil 2:25) "brother," and Phoebe (Rom 16:1) and Apphia (Phlm 2) "sister." From these instances it appears Paul has taken an everyday familial relationship term and used it in a heightened sense. Whereas in secular society siblings come from the "womb" (*delphus*) of the mother, in Paul's use, "brothers" and "sisters" are part of a family that come from a Godly womb! Is it not possible that Paul partnered *adelphēn* with *gynaika* in 1 Corinthians 9:5 to accentuate the richness of the gift he is willing to forgo for the benefit of others? And, remember, he has already experienced the gift of a good marriage while he lived with Priscilla and Aquila. It is a gift that the Corinthians to whom he writes had also witnessed.

Writing at the end of the second century CE, Clement of Alexandria understood 1 Corinthians 9:5 as a reference to spiritual marriage, so he embellished the text: "and they took their wives with them not as women with whom they had marriage relations but as sisters that they might be their co-missionaries in dealing with housewives" (*Miscellanies* 3.6.53.3). By then, his reading was appropriate; but it was not in the time of Paul.[15] Besides, Carolyn Osiek and Margaret Y. MacDonald think it is difficult to harmonize the "spiritual marriage" interpretation of 1 Corinthians 9:5 with Paul's strong rejection of perpetual celibacy within marriage in 1 Corinthians 7:2-5.[16] Having said all this, the translators of the RSV best capture Paul's statement, within the context of giving up rights and freedoms for the benefit of others: "Do [I] not have the right to be accompanied by a wife?" Of particular interest to me is the rest of this verse: "as the other apostles and the brothers of the Lord and Cephas," for surely Mark 1:30 tells us Peter had a mother-in-law.

In sum, since the legal capacity for marriage in the Roman Empire existed between two free citizens and was ruled out completely for slaves, it must mean Priscilla and Aquila are two free people who married.

(2) Recently Expelled from Rome

Dating Claudius' expulsion. Aquila and Priscilla travel to Corinth because "as Judeans" they were among the people Claudius deported from Rome on account of riots, which he would have viewed as an egregious "disorder." The Latin historian Suetonius refers to this event in his *Life of Claudius*, which he wrote in the first third of the second century. But while he says, "Claudius expelled Judeans from Rome who were constantly making disturbances at the instigation of Chrestus"

(25.4), he does not give us a date for the expulsion edict. A later fifth-century Christian historian does, placing Claudius' expulsion edict in the ninth year of his reign (January 25, 49 CE–January 24, 50 CE; cf. Paulus Orosius, *Historiae adversum paganos* 7.6.15-16). It is the date with which most scholars agree.

Those who differ with this date point to a second text that they think also records an imperial expulsion. This one happened in 41 CE. Their suggestion is based on a remark Dio Cassius makes in his *Roman History* 60.6.6. For here in reporting an action Claudius took against the Judeans in Rome at the beginning of his principate, Dio says: "As for the Judeans who had again increased so greatly that by reason of their multitude it would have been hard without raising a tumult to bar them from the city, he did not drive them out, but ordered them, while continuing their traditional mode of life, not to hold meetings." It is an unsustainable reference since no Judeans were expelled at this time. Instead, they were merely forbidden from gathering for meetings since Claudius thought they could be a source of unrest.[17] The fact that Dio Cassius makes no mention of Chrestos is a further obstacle to identifying 41 CE as the date for Luke's reference.[18] Both dates are linked, however, for surely, after Claudius saw that his prior leniency had done nothing to create order in 41 CE, he reacted more severely in 49 CE. This time, he expelled people.

Placing the expulsion at 49 CE also coheres with Paul's visit to Corinth (50/51 CE), which would have happened soon after Priscilla and Aquila arrived there. In fact, Luke's use of *prosphatōs* (recently; cf. Acts 18:2) sets up a chronological relationship between the couple's arrival and that of Paul, so neatly that both Ernst Haenchen and Luke Timothy Johnson claim Paul's meeting up with them provides a fixed point of reference for a very uncertain Pauline chronology.[19] This year also fits well with the generally accepted dating of Gallio's proconsulship of Achaia before whom Paul appears in Acts 18:12 (51/52 CE, see n. 1 above). It also fits into the period within which Claudius engaged in a campaign to restore the old Roman rites and, at the same time, check the growth of foreign cults (47–52 CE).[20]

How many people were expelled? Several details of Luke's account of Claudius' expulsion need to be addressed. The first is the question of numbers, since Luke claims Claudius commanded *all the Judeans* to leave Rome. As it is estimated there were between forty to fifty thousand Judeans living in Rome by the time of Augustus, his assertion is astonishing.[21] Moreover, had numbers such as these been deported, both Suetonius and Josephus would have noted it. Besides, one must take into account Luke's penchant for using rhetorical hyperbole in both his gospel and Acts, since it is his way of underlining the importance of something. As such, Harry J. Leon is correct when he asserts that "although some trouble-making groups were banished from the city under Tiberius and Claudius, there was never any general expulsion of Judeans from Rome."[22] Instead, only the chief leaders in the dispute that arose in 49 CE were banned, which is a manageable and less reportable number. In truth, Claudius probably didn't even know that among those he expelled there were some Judean Christ believers, for at this point no one in authority knew the difference (cf. Acts 16:20). Yet there were, for as Tertullian later observed, until the time of Nero the church grew under the shadow of the synagogue (cf. *Apol.* 21).

Chrestos: *Person or point of faith?* Undoubtedly, the Judeans Claudius expelled were the leaders of contending factions within the synagogue. They were, as Suetonius relates, rioting "at the instigation of Chrestus" (*impulsore Chresto*). It is a behavior Luke will recount many times in his narrative. But who or what is *Chrestus* (pronounced "Christos")? Is he an otherwise unknown agitator who was active in Judean circles in the 40s in Rome? Hardly, since among the 550 names Leon lists as used by Judeans in Rome in the first century, *Chrestus* is not among them.[23] Or, is Suetonius referring to the trouble that arose in the Judean community as a result of Judean Christ followers preaching that Jesus of Nazareth was the Messiah/*Christos* of God, the anointed one in their synagogues?

F. F. Bruce does not think *Chrestus* refers to an unknown agitator since if he were, Suetonius would have called him "a certain"

Chrestus, as he would be singling him out as an individual.[24] Instead, what we have is the careless spelling of the name *Christus*, which is the equivalent of the Hebrew title "Messiah." In fact, there is evidence that *Chrestus/Chrēstos* and *Chrestiani* were misspellings for *Christus/Christos* and *Christiani/Christianoi*, in both Latin and Greek for the first few centuries. Tacitus, for example, knew the *Chrestianoi* and that their name came from the word *Christus* (*Ann* 15.44.4), and Tertullian tells us that even in the early third century the common pronunciation for *Christus* and *Christianos* was *Chrestus* and *Chrestianos* (*Apol* 3). Thus, Suetonius was probably referring to Jesus Christ, but he had misunderstood his sources. For although Tacitus knew that Christ was executed under Tiberius, Suetonius did not have the same concern for historical precision. So, if his sources told him that the rioting among Judeans in Rome was caused by disagreement about the claims of Christ, it was natural, if mistaken, for him to believe that Christ was in Rome at that time.[25] Instead, the riots (disorder) Suetonius reports, "at the instigation of Chrestus," were the result of Judean Christ believers' preaching the Messiahship of Jesus in one or more of the synagogues of the city. Disorder ensued. Such a scenario

> is no different from what is attested for synagogues in Jerusalem (Acts 6:9-15), Antioch in Pisidia (13:45, 50), Iconia (14:2, 5), Lystra (14:19), and Corinth (18:12-17). Followers of the Christ message were therefore involved in synagogal conflicts. They—as members of synagogues—were the first urban Roman Christians. [26]

Priscilla and Aquila were among them. Furthermore, since banishment seems to have applied only to the leaders and activists, it is safe to assume that both Priscilla and Aquila were particularly active on the Judean Christ believers side. As Wolfgang Wiefel notes:

> Since Rome had no supervising body which could forbid any form of Christian propaganda in the city, it was pos-

sible to missionize in various synagogues concurrently or to go successively from one to another. It is likely that the existence of newly converted Christians alongside the traditional members of the synagogue may have led to increased factions and even to tumultuous disputes.[27]

These eruptions occurred because the preaching of these Judean Christ believers would have been viewed as blasphemous by some of the mainstream Judeans; as the person they preached as God's Messiah had been crucified. Accordingly, their assertion was impossible, for the law of Moses stated that anyone who was put to death by hanging (which would include crucifixion) would be cursed by God (cf. Deut 21:22-23). Rioting followed. Such conflict spelled disorder. It was something the Romans sought to avoid at all costs.

Has Luke shown us that Aquila and Priscilla were Christ believers before they met Paul? Luke never mentions that Aquila and Priscilla were believers in Christ before they arrived in Corinth. We could never expect that he would, since by mentioning this detail he would have to admit there was an active following of Jesus in Corinth before Paul arrived there. Yet, internal evidence within his text supports the assertion that Priscilla and Aquila were already believers in Christ before they left Rome.

While the later appearances of this couple in Acts clearly show they are believers (18:18, 26), Luke never refers to their baptism. Such an omission is odd since he usually mentions the conversion and baptism of prominent persons (cf. 2:41; 9:18; 8:36-39; 10:48; 16:15; etc.). His failure to do so in this instance must mean he knew they were baptized but saw no need to mention it.[28] Interestingly, Paul doesn't include an account of baptizing them either. Instead, he tells us that in Corinth he baptized only Gaius, Cripsus, and the household of Stephanus (1 Cor 1:14-16), and that Stephanus and his household were the "first converts of Achaea" (1 Cor 16:15). Surely, had Priscilla and Aquila needed to be baptized, he would have mentioned it; and especially since he both lived and worked with them (Acts 18:3). It is also more improbable that a Judean couple expelled because of the conflict with Judeans in Rome deliberately gave a Christ-believing missionary work and shelter (as they will do and perhaps later do for Apollos; cf. Acts 18:16) than that Paul found lodgings with Judean Christ believers who were expelled from Rome.[29] Likewise, if they are already believers, one can see why Paul both took and left this couple at Ephesus to lay some foundations for his later evangelistic work there (Acts 18:19). Why, Luke even tells us they enhanced Apollos' understanding (v. 26). So while Luke is silent about much of what Priscilla and Aquila do as missionaries, a hint of what they actually did in Corinth may be detected in his treatment of the establishment of the church at Ephesus. For while Luke makes Paul preach the first sermon (Acts 18:19-21), he clearly shows that Priscilla and Aquila established a community there (vv. 26-27) before Paul returned to take up residence and assume responsibility for the church (19:1-10).[30]

Might it also be possible that when Luke says Aquila is a Judean, a native of Pontus, he is also telling us Aquila was a Judean Christ believer? Several facts support this claim. First, *ioudaioi* from the Pontus area were among those who gathered in Jerusalem on the day of Pentecost (Acts 2:9). Later, Christ believers from Pontus were addressed by the author of 1 Peter (cf. 1:1; "To the exiles of the Dispersion in Pontus . . ."). From these two references it would appear that the Judeans from Pontus who were among those who gathered in Jerusalem for the feast of Pentecost must have returned home to spread the faith; and that they were successful. Perhaps Aquila may even have been one of their converts?

Second, Luke often uses the term *ioudaioi* when he is referring to Judean Christ believers. For example, when Paul and Silas are brought before the magistrates in Philippi, they are called *ioudaioi*, and we surely know they are Judean Christ believers (cf. Acts 16:20). Finally, Luke introduces Apollos in the same way he introduces Aquila only a few lines further: "Now a [Judean; *ioudaios*] named Apollos, a native of Alexandria" (Acts 18:24). That Apollos is "well versed in the scriptures . . . instructed in the way of the Lord . . . [and] spoke and taught accurately the things concerning Jesus" (Acts 18:24b-25) bespeaks of his being a Judean Christ believer. Besides, there is nowhere else in Acts that we find a Judean who is said to have been instructed in the things of the Lord and who is teaching accurately the things about Jesus who is *not* also a believer.[31]

Keeping all of this in mind, Claudius' edict may be our earliest evidence for the presence of the Messianic movement in Rome by the middle of the first century.[32] It may even tell us more about Aquila and Priscilla than Paul or Luke does; for we have already seen they were independent and original missionaries among their fellow Judeans even before they met Paul. Likewise, one can justifiably posit that their readiness to offer hospitality to Paul and a room for worship in their house both in Corinth and Ephesus is but a continuation of what they had already done in Rome before they were banished. Indeed, from the beginning, and in every way possible, Priscilla and Aquila were leaders and activists for the cause of Christ and the gospel.

(3) Who Relocate in Corinth as Tentmakers and/or Leatherworkers

During the New Testament era, residents of the Roman Empire traveled the Mediterranean region by both land and sea with an ease that would not appear again until the nineteenth century. Good travel conditions were the result of two things: an artery of roads that connected all the provinces and cities of the empire, making troop relocations easier, and a peace that was brought about and maintained by the Romans. This *Pax Romana*, among other things, curbed piracy.

Sea travel was faster and cheaper than travel by land but it was locked into a time frame that extended from late March to October.[33] Afterward, ships were taken out of service and remained docked until the following spring to avoid winter storms. It is likely Priscilla and Aquila walked the Appian Way to Brindisi. From there they went to Corinth by boat (late spring–early fall) and arrived at the port of Lechaeon. Perhaps other expelled Judean Christ believers (such as some of those mentioned in Rom 16) traveled with them, for they would all be looking for a place to live and practice their faith until they could go back to Rome. Besides, Corinth was an ideal place for both Priscilla and Aquila to ply their trade. It was a very populous place, and, as such, there would be constant needs for awnings for private houses and for shops in the forum, as well as for tents used for market booths. Furthermore, as the Isthmian Games were celebrated in the spring of 49 CE there would be a need for temporary lodgings for its visitors. Consequently, if Priscilla and Aquila arrived beforehand, they would be employed making tents; but if they arrived afterward there was still plenty to do, since repairs on used tents would be necessary. New tents would also need to be made as the next games were only fifteen months away.[34]

Tentmakers/Leatherworkers. Skēnopoios is a *hapax legomenon* in the New Testament, which means it is a word that is used only once in the texts. In its basic sense *skēnopoios* describes a person who makes tents, but in a wider sense, it also denotes an artisan who worked with either linen, canvas, or leather.[35] Early interpreters, such as John Chrysostom and Origen, believed that Paul, who refers to his labor but never to a specific trade (cf. 1 Thess 2:9; 1 Cor 4:12), worked with leather, as Priscilla and Aquila did. Later scholars thought they worked with linen and canvas.[36] Ivoni Richter Reimer disputes their claim since she thinks it is based on a faulty premise. Its theorists thought that as Paul came from Tarsus in Cilicia and the rough cloth woven of goats' hair (*cilicium*) was also made there, he must have both made and used this product since he learned how to weave in Tarsus. Indeed, local Bedouins, called "Skenites," used goat hair for making tents as well. Reimer counters their theory, arguing the following: (1) *cilicium* is not synonymous with *skēne*, and (2) as it stems only from Paul's home country, Aquila and Priscilla could not have used it. Yet, according to Acts 18:3, Paul not only carried on this trade, but Priscilla and Aquila did so with him.[37] Furthermore, as Brian M. Rapske suggests:

If Paul's overland journeys were generally undertaken by foot, the recently popular explanation of Acts 18:3 that Paul was a weaver of tentcloth made from goat's hair or linen, whatever its other problems, is rendered even less probable. Such an occupation, requiring tools and equipment inconvenient in size, weight and shape, is hardly in keeping with the impression in Acts of a highly mobile Paul—even less so a pedestrian Paul. The maker/repairer of tents and other leather products, carrying his bag of cutting tools, awls, sharpening stone and such, presents a more consistent and more credible picture.[38]

Today most scholars think all three missionaries worked with leather, and they picture the three of them working for long hours, bent forward on a stool by a workbench.[39] All that was needed was a set of basic tools, which included round-edge and straight-edge knives to cut the leather and awls, needles, and thread to sew it. So little was necessary, it made "tenting" a portable thriving trade. Indeed, Acts 28:30 may even imply Paul worked when he was in custody in Rome. More onerous was the abundance of strength and patience that were also needed, for as Paul later comments, "We grow weary from the work of our own hands" (1 Cor 4:12; NRSV). Yet he was willing to work "night and day, that we might not burden any of you, while we preached to you the gospel of God" (1 Thess 2:9). It is a price he was willing to pay from the very beginning of his ministry. For when he asks in 1 Corinthians 9:6, "Or is it only Barnabas and I who have no right to refrain from working for a living?" one must remember that the only time these two men traveled together was on his first missionary journey.

Murphy-O'Connor spells out "tentings" endless as well as destructive potential:

Tentmakers were equally at home in sewing together strips of leather or different weights of canvas. There is little difference in technique in joining two thicknesses of leather or layers of heavy canvas. It takes an awl to make the hole in a rolled-over canvas seam just as it does in leather, and

in both cases the needle must be slipped through before
the hole closes. It is but a short step to sewing leather
cloaks, belts and gourds, all equipment of the traveler. Since
skill was more important than strength, women could sew
as well as men. Inevitably, a tentmaker developed muscular
shoulders and strong, calloused hands. The stitch was set
by a sudden outward jerk of both hands into which the
thread bit.[40]

Surprisingly, although *skēnopoios* performed a necessary task, they
were despised as a trade since what they did was considered a
demeaning manual labor. Paul mentions this fact himself: "You
are held in honor, but we in disrepute. To the present hour we
hunger and thirst, we are ill-clad and buffeted and homeless, and
we labor, working with our own hands. When reviled, we bless"
(1 Cor 4:10c-12). In Priscilla and Aquila's case, however, their occupation was a sweet endeavor; for at first, with both strength and
skill, these refugees practiced their art together. *But not for long!*

(4) With Whom Paul Lived and Worked

A triad of workers, a triad of workings. Paul's preaching in Athens
brings mixed results. For while some people like Dionysius, a
member of the court of the Areopagus, became a believer, "as did
Damaris and the others with them" (Acts 17:34), other listeners
did not. In fact, some of them scoffed at him, while others post-
poned a decision which is a response according to Acts that is
equivalent to unbelief (cf. Acts 24:25). As such, Paul may have left
Athens a disheartened missionary. Yet in the plan of God a surprise
awaited him. For in Corinth, he met a couple who shared not only
the same trade with him but their home and their faith as well. It
was an unbeatable triad and part of the hundredfold the gospel
promises (cf. Mark 10:30). Moreover, Luke tells us Aquila, Priscilla,
and Paul worked together. So despite the fact that some commentators, like the Western Text (D),[41] W. Michaelis,[42] Ronald F. Hock,[43]
and Peter Lampe,[44] have eliminated Priscilla, the construction,
continuity, and the grammatical structure of Luke's text tell us they

were a trio. "He [Paul] stayed *with them* [Aquila and Priscilla], and *they* worked, for by trade *they* were tentmakers" (Acts 18:3; emphasis added). As such, there is no good reason to exclude Priscilla from the "they/them" team. Moreover, the portrayal of Paul as "working" with Aquila and Priscilla can reasonably be inferred from 1 Corinthians 4:12a. As here in using the same verb that appears in Acts 18:3, Paul speaks of "working with our own hands," and its plural forms suggest that he engaged in such work in collaboration with one or more people.

Aquila and Priscilla's dwelling and economic status. The remains of a vaulted shop in Corinth's *agora* stir my imagination. I envisage it as the workshop/home of Priscilla and Aquila. This particular two-storied edifice conforms to the type of place artisans rented at that time. Its lower level provided space to practice trade (storage space for different weights and widths of leather and linen and a narrow bench for each worker, plus access to the street), while its upper story, created by a wooden platform halfway up to divide the room into two levels, afforded living quarters.[45]

The shop pictured above is centrally located; but wherever theirs was, little shops like this were scattered all over the city.

A workshop could be located almost anywhere. A room in
an artisan's house could serve as a workshop, as could a
ground floor room in an apartment building, with the
artisan living in an upstairs room, in a back room, or even
in the back of the shop itself. Or a workshop could be located in a separate building.[46]

Most often, however, shops were located on busy streets and
in places in or near the *agora*, or marketplace, for these were
places that would attract business.

That two independent artisans were able to extend hospitality
to Paul suggests Priscilla and Aquila did not operate at a subsis-
tence level; but this scarcely places them among the elite. In fact,
John Chrysostom, the first great commentator of Acts, depicts
them as "poor and living by the work of their hands," as do other
early church writers.[47] Paul's own testimony confirms this picture:
"And when I was with you [in Corinth] and was in want, I did
not burden any one, for my needs were supplied by the brethren
who came from Macedonia" (2 Cor 11:9). It is a need Paul finds
humiliating (2 Cor 11:7; cf. 1 Cor 4:11-13). It is also why Priscilla
worked, since wives were often required to assist their husbands
in difficult manual trades, simply to make ends meet.[48] Not everyone agrees with this picture, as scholars like Ernst Haenchen,
Gerd Theissen, Rudolf Pesch, and Hans-Josef Klauck think Priscilla and Aquila are a well-to-do couple.[49] Meeks does as well.[50]
Reimer disagrees, contending (a) inscriptional, (b) archaeological,
and (c) Pauline material (such as has been indicated throughout
this chapter) challenge their "well-to-do entrepreneur" thesis.[51]

Inscriptional material indicates that in comparison to the actual percentage of the population, artisans of Aquila's stamp are
underrepresented in the inscriptions. This is because their trade
enjoyed so little prestige.[52] As Lampe observes:

In Roman epitaphs, for example, relatively few handworkers are mentioned who are in the private sector, that is,
those who exercise their trade apart from the "familia Cae-
saris" or the state. Among the 10,892 persons mentioned
in the inscriptions, only 72 are recognizable as some kind

of craftsman of the private sector. That is less than one percent. In comparison to their actual proportion in the population (presumably considerably more than double as many), handworkers of Aquila's kind are under-represented in the inscriptions.[53]

Excavations at Corinth also shed light on the size of work-room/shops or workshop/houses of artisans. Lampe claims these excavations confirm that smaller individual shops were a little more than three meters wide and their length a little less than four meters, while larger shops were four and a half meters wide and six meters long.[54] In American terms this means shop rooms were generally eight to fourteen feet wide and twelve to twenty-four feet deep. As such, Priscilla and Aquila probably lived in the loft, lit by an unglazed window centered above the shop's entrance, while Paul slept below amid the tool-strewn workbenches and rolls of leather and canvas.[55]

This arrangement worked for Paul at the beginning of his time in Corinth, since he could work while holding important con-versations with customers or with others who dropped by. No doubt Priscilla and Aquila assisted him. Yet their efforts are no more recounted than are the missionary efforts of Silas and Timo-thy; but that is not to deny them.[56] Moreover, their home was probably the place where believers met, as they probably did before Paul arrived. Murphy-O'Connor envisions the downstairs room where they gathered:

> It was not luxurious, but it was clean, and the leather and canvas stacked against the wall served as improvised couches. Others sat on the benches or stools. Children were ranged on the ladder. Depending on the size of the room, the assembly numbered between 10 and 20 believers. In winter it must have been rather cozy. The shutters were closed against the biting wind, and the brazier gave both light and warmth. In summer it was a different matter. The shutters could not be left open without attracting the un-welcome attention of the street. The flickering flames of oil lamps intensified the heat of the airless crowded room.

Such discomfort, however, mattered little to those whose
sharing of bread and wine brought Christ into their midst.[57]

As time went on, the numbers increased. This was partly because, having received aid from Macedonia (2 Cor 11:9; Phil 4:14-
15), Paul no longer needed to work and was able to give his entire
attention to the mission (Acts 18:5) instead of only preaching on
the Sabbath (v. 4). Consequently, he needed a larger space to evangelize, since the room the young couple provided could hold no
more than twenty people. So, after he left the synagogue, he moved
his preaching activities into the house of Titius Justus, a "god-
fearer" (i.e., a non-Judean synagogue adherent) who had presumably become a believer. Besides, his house was located next to the
synagogue (Acts 18:7). Notice it is never said that Aquila and Priscilla owned a house. In fact, Lampe claims, their move from
Corinth after eighteen months (Acts 18:11) indicates they did not
possess real estate in Corinth, since it would have held them back.[58]
Instead they rented a workshop-residence that was available for
just such craftspeople. Indeed, that Priscilla and Aquila's home,
in Corinth as well as in Ephesus, does not come into question as
the place for a great gathering of listeners further supports the
picture of average craftspeople of lower social status.

In sum, Priscilla and Aquila belong to that very populous
lower order of minor craftspeople in Corinth who earned their
living with their own hands. What they earned was not ex-
travagant but it must have been more than sufficient since they
were able to extend help to those who were less well-off than
themselves.

Scene Two: Acts 18:18-19

*After this [these things] Paul stayed many days longer, and then
took leave of the brethren and sailed for Syria, and with him Priscilla
and Aquila. At Cenchreae he cut his hair, for he had a vow. And they
came to Ephesus, and he left them there.*

"After This [These Things]" Context

Eighteen months lie between verses 1-3 and 18-19 of Acts 18. In between, Paul lived and worked with Priscilla and Aquila (18:1-3), and he preached in the synagogue every Sabbath (18:4), until he was no longer allowed in it (18:6). Like the Judean Christ preachers in the synagogues in Rome, Paul's message that Jesus was the Messiah of God resulted in intense opposition (cf. Suetonius, *Claudius*, 25.4). In response, he departed and moved his evangelistic outreach into the home of Titius Justus. At this point, the Western Text (D) proposes Paul moved out of Aquila's house (notice how Priscilla was dropped), but this is unlikely since the ties that developed between them were too deep to sever. More likely, he only moved his venue for preaching from the synagogue to a larger private house. Not everyone appreciated Paul's efforts, and he was brought before Gallio, the Roman governor (vv. 12-17), to the *bema*, a raised area in the marketplace which was used for rendering judgments. Surely Priscilla and Aquila were nearby to support him.

Understandably, members of the synagogue were his critics since they were threatened by his words and the effect they seemed to have on their leaders such as Crispus (1 Cor 1:14). They charged that Paul was persuading people to worship God contrary to the law, i.e., he was preaching a faith that was not recognized "by Rome" and hence was a threat to her best interests. But Gallio, realizing their charge was an internal matter, brought the proceedings to an end. In effect, he granted Paul and his fledgling group the same protection that Roman law granted to the practice of Judaism.[59] Might Luke have told this story as an example of the truth of the words he reported just before this (Acts 18:9-10): "And the Lord said to Paul one night in a vision, 'Do not be afraid, but speak [go on speaking, as the Greek tense suggests] and do not be silent; *for I am with you*, and no [one] shall attack you to harm you'" (emphasis added)? And so "after these things" and with renewed assurance (which is a very big concept in Luke-Acts [cf. *asphelia* in Luke 1:1-4]), "Paul stayed many days longer [in partnership ministry with Priscilla and Aquila]" (Acts 18:18).

"And They Came to Ephesus, and He Left Them There"

It would appear that Paul was ready to move from Corinth when he thought others within the Corinthian Christ believers could continue what he, Priscilla, and Aquila had begun. We learn later from 1 Corinthians, however, that although this community lasted they divided into smaller groups (cf. 1 Cor 1–4) and that they needed his pastoral hand from afar. Indeed, at the end of the letter he wrote to them, Paul singled out Stephanas who put his house and household (which presumably includes women) at their service, and he urged this fractured community to be subject to them and to every fellow worker and laborer (1 Cor 16:15f.). Surely this is because as "fellow workers" of Paul their concern would not have been for themselves but for others.

Murphy-O'Connor suggests Paul's move to Ephesus was part of his missionary strategy:

> His churches arched from Galatia in the east to Corinth in
> the west; Ephesus lay at the center. It was the obvious choice

and his next missionary target, and the fact that it was roughly equidistant from all his other communities meant that he could stay in touch with them easily. Paul's experience at Corinth had made him aware of the advantage of having a base already prepared when he arrived.[60]

And so, it would seem when he wanted to go to Antioch, where he began his second missionary journey with Silas (Acts 15:40), he asked Priscilla and Aquila to accompany him and to do there (which they will do, cf. 1 Cor 16:19) what they had already done in Corinth before he arrived there. Later he would return to them (Acts 19:1). Were Priscilla and Aquila to agree to his plan it would be a sacrifice because they would lose whatever trade they had managed to build up in Corinth. But, committed to God and the gospel, they left everything and accompanied him 250 miles across the Aegean Sea to Ephesus. While Corinth was large, Ephesus was huge, with a population of a quarter of a million people.[61] It was the third largest city in the Roman Empire (behind Rome and Alexandria) and the capital and greatest commercial city of the Roman province of Asia. It was also the largest city Paul visited during his missionary activity, excluding Rome. In addition, the renowned Temple of Artemis was located there, and as it was regarded as one of the Seven Wonders of the World, it attracted many pilgrims. It was also home to a significant Judean population (cf. Josephus, *Ant.* 14.225-27; 16.162-68, 172-73).

Luke again positions Paul as the initiator of a new mission. So, before he leaves Ephesus he records that Paul went to the synagogue and argued with the Judeans (Acts 18:19), after which he leaves (18:18-23) and doesn't return until chapter 19, when he probably lived again with Priscilla and Aquila. For later when he writes to the Corinthian church from Ephesus, he will include their greetings in his letter (1 Cor 16:19). While he is gone, Priscilla and Aquila evangelize (Acts 18:26) and are functioning much like Barnabas, Timothy, Silas, and other Pauline missionary partners.[62]

Scene Three: Acts 18:26-27

He [Apollos] began to speak boldly in the synagogue; but when Priscilla and Aquila heard him, they took him and expounded to him the way of God more accurately. And when he wished to cross to Achaia, the brethren encouraged him, and wrote to the disciples to receive him.

The only activity Luke reports about Priscilla and Aquila's evangelistic endeavors is that they taught Apollos, a Judean native of Alexandria, whom he depicts as an "eloquent man, well versed in the scriptures" (18:24). It is a description that comports with Apollos' having come from Alexandria; since it was a place that was known for its learning and philosophical reflection. Part of his instruction had been "in the way of the Lord" (18:25a). By saying this, Luke means Apollos had received formal instruction about Jesus; for here, as elsewhere in Acts, "Lord" refers to Jesus. The phrase "in the way of the Lord" then explains the verse that follows it, which indicates how Apollos could accurately teach the things about Jesus. Since:

> V. 28 likely makes clear at least part of what is meant by this latter phrase, namely that he was able to show from the Hebrew Scriptures that the Messiah was Jesus. This is partly confirmed by the fact that already in v. 24, before he ever met Priscilla and Aquila, Apollos is said to be "powerful in the writings of Scripture," which from Luke's Christian point of view means precisely that he was able to use them Christologically in an effective manner (cf. Lk 24: 44-49).[63]

At this point, Luke's positive assessment ends, as he tells us (with regret) that Apollos "knew only the baptism of John" (Acts 18:25c). As such, there was a deficiency in his understanding of the gospel. It is a lacuna Priscilla and Aquila catch upon hearing him boldly speak in the synagogue and they respond as good missionaries would, since "they took him [aside] and expounded to him the way of God more accurately" (v. 26b). In fact, they shared Paul's theological outlook with Apollos, which is an assertion Paul implies later in 1 Corinthians 3:5-9.

That Priscilla is named first may suggest she is Apollos' main tutor as John Chrysostom puts forward in his First Homily on the Greeting to Priscilla and Aquila:

> Paul has placed Priscilla before her husband. For he does not say, "Greet Aquila and Priscilla," but "Priscilla and Aquila." He does not do this without a reason, but he seems to acknowledge a greater godliness for her than for her husband. What I said is not guess-work, because, it is possible to learn this from the Book of Acts. She took Apollos, an eloquent man and powerful in the Scriptures, but knowing only the baptism of John; and she instructed him in the way of the Lord and made him a teacher brought to completion (Acts 18:24-25).[64]

The Western Text, however, followed by other writers, changed the order from "Priscilla and Aquila" to "Aquila and Priscilla." Whatever the case, that Apollos was not just any convert to the faith but as Luke says a man "well versed in the scriptures" (Acts 18:24) demonstrates that both of these people were knowledgeable enough to teach this teacher, and their competence is confirmed by his later success in Corinth (cf. 1 Cor 3:6). In fact, when reflecting on this scene, John Chrysostom says, "He sailed to Syria . . . and with him Priscilla—Lo, a woman also—and Aquila. But he left these at Ephesus. With good reason, namely that they should teach" (Homily 40 on the Acts of the Apostles [18:18]).

Priscilla and Aquila also show their diplomatic and pastoral sense in that, instead of challenging him publicly, they took him aside privately, perhaps to their home. Obviously, their teaching was effective, for when Apollos wished to move on to Achaia,[65] "the brethren [i.e., those converted by the brief appearance of Paul, or more likely from the ministry of Priscilla and Aquila, for as we learn in 1 Cor 16:19 they met as a house church in their home] encouraged him and wrote [a letter] to the disciples [in Corinth] to receive him" (Acts 18:27). Surely, the names of Priscilla and Aquila in this letter spoke volumes, for letters were a form of presence, and the Corinthians already knew and trusted this couple.[66]

Priscilla and Aquila's Impact on the Lives and Faith of the Early Believers according to Acts

It would appear that having spent some time with this couple we have discovered there is more to Priscilla and Aquila than Luke's introduction of them first suggested. For here we merely learned they were: (1) a married couple (2) recently expelled from Rome (3) who relocated in Corinth as tentmakers and/or leatherworkers and (4) with whom Paul lived and worked (Acts 18:2). If we were to ask someone to describe them based on this description, we would end up with something like this: This is a hospitable, artisan couple, who, despite adversity, was able to move on and share their home, faith, and trade with Paul.

Having explored Luke's words, and their surrounding context, and supported by his other snippets concerning them, let us now consider a new way to think about them. (1) Priscilla and Aquila were *active Judean Christ believers and leaders* in Rome and Corinth before they met Paul. Indeed, their initial work in Corinth made it easier for his missionary activity when he arrived there; however, Luke chooses to be silent about it. (2) Paul trusted them and they supported each other not only financially but spiritually as well, for surely through the eighteen months they were together their many conversations and prayer times enabled them all to stay focused despite the growing opposition. (3) Later Paul included them in his plans to further the mission when he left Corinth, and they, as *missionaries* (a term Luke never applies to them), left everything to be part of it. (4) From the start, this "triad" were *coworkers in Christ Jesus.* In truth, Paul left them "in charge" in Ephesus when he moved on to Antioch, Galatia, and Phrygia, and to do there what they had already done in Corinth. If we were to ask someone to describe Priscilla and Aquila based on this description, we would end up with something like this: Priscilla and Aquila were (1) a missionary couple (2) who as active Judean Christ believers (3) and leaders and teachers in Rome, Corinth, and Ephesus (4) were coworkers, founders, and leaders with Paul of various Jesus groups for the cause of Christ. And although Paul emphatically states he planted the seed (1 Cor 3:6), "laid a foundation" (1 Cor 3:10), and begot the Corinthians in Christ Jesus through his preaching of the gospel (1 Cor 4:15b), which are all part of the argument he makes later in an attempt to unify the community (cf. 1 Cor 1:10-4:21) after he (and Priscilla and Aquila) had left them, I am convinced that the "origins" of the Corinthian group began in a small way with Priscilla and Aquila, along with the other Judean Christ believers who were expelled from Rome and who relocated with them in Corinth. These nascent believers must have frequently gathered together to nurture their faith and in so doing provided an example to their neighbors that piqued their interest and encouraged them to give Paul a hearing when he arrived there. *They were a presence that strengthened!*

CHAPTER 2

The Testimony of Paul
(1 Cor 16:19; Rom 16:3-5)
and Deutero-Paul (2 Tim 4:19)

Having learned a great deal about Priscilla and Aquila based on the writings of one who did not know them, we now will examine the writings of one who did (1 Cor 16:19; Rom 16:3-5). We will also review the text of a person who wrote long after Paul died and who wrote in his name (2 Tim 4:19). In each case, we will examine the what, when, and where of the text, highlight its backdrop, and draw some conclusions. The significance of the "house church" and its contribution to the development and expansion of the early Jesus groups will also be addressed.

A. The Testimony of Paul

1 Corinthians 16:19

The churches of Asia [i.e., in the Roman province of Asia] send greetings [to you Corinthians]. Aquila and Prisca, together with the church in their house, send you hearty greetings in the Lord.

The World of Aquila and Prisca[1]

Paul writes a few lines of greetings in the closing chapter of his "first" letter to the Corinthian church, written from Ephesus in the midfifties.[2] It is the place Luke tells us to which Paul, Aquila, and Prisc(ill)a went after leaving Corinth (Acts 18:18f.). It would appear Paul left this couple here as an advance team while he went to Antioch, Galatia, and Phrygia (Acts 18:21). Later he rejoined them (Acts 19:1). While he was gone, Priscilla and Aquila attended the synagogue, preached about Jesus the Messiah, taught Apollos (as they no doubt taught others), and continued their practice of hosting a church in their home. It was probably the house church in Ephesus to which Paul himself was attached.[3] The Corinthian community would be especially receptive to Aquila and Prisc(ill)a's greetings since the very mention of their names would remind them of the many experiences they had shared in Corinth. Most likely, many of them had attended services in their home which John Chrysostom later notes showed "no small excellency" in their regard (Homily 44 on First Corinthians, v. 19). By reminding the Corinthian believers of this association, Paul connected the Ephesian and

Corinthian communities. First Corinthians 16:19 also reminds us that the early believers met in private homes. Indeed, for more than two hundred years domestic dwellings shaped the early believers' community and religious life.

At this point, it may be helpful to examine the importance and function of the house church (what it is) and determine the activities Prisc(ill)a and Aquila were probably associated with in Corinth, Ephesus, and Rome (what a house church does).

What a House Church Is

Although Acts of the Apostles tells us that the early followers of Jesus assembled in houses (cf. 2:46; 5:42; etc.), the first missionary use of a house is mentioned by Mark, and it is used by Jesus himself: "And when he returned to Capernaum after some days, it was reported that he was at home. And many were gathered together, so that there was no longer room for them, not even about the door; and he was preaching the word to them" (Mark 2:1-2). Jesus used houses as a location for teaching many times (Mark 3:19b-20; 7:17; cf. 4:10-13; 9:28; 10:1-12; etc.). Later, his disciples used houses themselves, and it is reasonable to assume that houses were one of the primary reasons for the spread of the gospel.[4] Time after time the New Testament gives examples of the apostles beginning their missionary work in a city by first winning households from which they could center their activities (cf. Acts 10:48; 16:15; 1 Cor 16:15). Concomitantly, the New Testament also implies the expansion of Jesus groups was so rapid that it required meeting in more than one house in the various locales (cf. 1 Cor 5:4; 14:23; 1 Thess 5:27; Rom 16:23).

Groups of believers in Jesus met in private homes, each constituting a "house church" (*hē kat' oikon ekklēsia*). The New Testament explicitly mentions four of them: in the house of Aquila and Prisca (1 Cor 16:19; Rom 16:5), in the house of Archippus (Phlm 2), and in the house of Nympha (Col 4:15). Houses were the first centers of church life. Inside these domestic dwellings, believers studied, prayed, and worshiped as a small group. Houses were also places for instruction, as they had been in

Jesus' day. Since they varied in size, so did the number of people that could meet in them. As time went on, and the number of believers increased, many small groups met in one area (cf. 1 Cor 1:12-13). On special occasions, they joined together as a "whole church" in a bigger space (1 Cor 14:23; Rom 16:23).

Houses and households were of fundamental importance to the burgeoning church. In a seminal article titled "The Significance of Early House Churches," Floyd Filson claims that the New Testament church would be better understood if more attention were paid to the actual physical conditions under which the early believers met and lived.[5] He then highlighted five contextual elements from which we could learn: (1) houses provided a setting where a distinct Christ-centered worship was celebrated and where early believers experienced the courage-sustaining fellowship of the group;[6] (2) household settings explain why so much attention was paid to family relationships both in the letters of Paul and in other early writings; (3) several house churches located in one city helps to explain the tendency to "party strife" in the apostolic age; (4) a study of the house church situation throws light on the social status of the earliest believers in Jesus as its makeup was a cross section of society, replicating the social mixture of any household community (i.e., from wealthy landowner to slave); (5) leaders emerged from house settings to succeed the apostolic workers. A brief overview of Filson's points is now in order.

(1) House Churches Provided the Setting
for a Distinct Worship and Fellowship

Houses provided a natural setting where the early believers could gather without dependence on the temple or synagogue styles. Here, they were free to develop patterns that authenticated their own beliefs and needs. The size and style of a house determined the number of people a house church could accommodate. For surely archaeology has shown both Palestinian as well as Hellenistic Roman houses run the gamut from the small home of the poor to the villa of the wealthy.

Palestinian housing. Acts tells us that for a time Judean Jesus believers continued to go to the temple for prayer (Acts 3:1), while "breaking bread in their homes" (Acts 2:46). They could not thrive within this institution (or for that matter, in the synagogue), however, without disturbing the peace; for like new wine in old wineskins, they no longer fit in them. Inevitably, Judean Jesus believers were no longer welcomed in either place. And so, having no meeting place of their own, they met in private houses, as did subsequent Jesus followers until Constantine began building the first basilicas throughout the empire in the fourth century.[7]

Houses varied in size according to the social status of their owners.[8] A Palestinian house of a poor family in a village, for example, would have difficulty accommodating believers since families lived on one floor in a square, box-like apartment. These dwellings were divided into two parts, one section being higher than the other. Livestock were kept in its lower level, while the family, with its scant belongings, occupied the upper portion of the house. It was their living room, dining room, and bedroom all rolled into one room. A flat roof on top of the house had many uses: sleeping, drying vegetables, ripening fruit, or saying one's prayers. While poorer dwellings in Jerusalem might not have had livestock, they would also have been very small. Consequently, only a few believers could gather in their space. Yet, believers must have, for in summarizing their communal life, Luke tells us, "And day by day, attending the temple together and breaking bread in their homes, they partook of food with glad and generous hearts" (Acts 2:46). In addition, believers didn't meet in just one house but in many homes (*kat' oikon*; cf. Acts 5:42). In fact, in describing Paul's persecution of the early believers, Luke says, "entering *house after house*, he [Paul] dragged off men and women" (Acts 8:3; emphasis added).

People of means, on the other hand, lived in multistoried houses. The *huperoon* was the second or third floor of this type of house. In the East it was also the most ventilated and best-furnished room, and it was given to any visitor whom its owner desired to honor.

> Such a room, was quite common in ancient architecture and was utilized in a variety of ways. In contrast to the lower, large-sized living room, upper rooms were not normally used for everyday activities (sleeping, cooking, eating, etc.).They were a place for rest and relaxation. Even as early as OT times they occasionally had a certain religious significance (1 Kgs 17:19-21; 2 Kgs 4:10-11; Dan 6:11). For this reason they became the preferred meeting place for scribes. Scholars used them not only as meeting rooms (*m, Šabb*.1:4; *y. Sanh.* 21b) but as study rooms (*b. Šabb*. 13b) and prayer rooms as well. In light of this ancient and Jewish usage, it appears quite plausible that the primitive church in Jerusalem would make use of an upper room as a gathering place just as Luke indicates in Acts 1:12-15.[9]

According to Luke, early believers used "upper rooms" as a place of assembly and prayer (Acts 1:12-15; cf. 2:1; 9:36-41; 12:12-17). They were also used as a place where guests (Acts 1:13) and later missionaries could stay. Guests could also come and go at will from this room, which was accessible via a stairway located outside the house. Undoubtedly, house hospitality was a major factor in the transmission of the gospel. We will examine Luke's references.

In Acts 1:12-15, we find the Eleven, along with the women (cf. Luke 23:55; 24:1, 9, 22), Mary the mother of Jesus, and his brothers staying in Jerusalem in a house with an upper room. Here they gathered for prayer and support (1:12-14), which the tense of the verbs indicates they did on an ongoing basis. Although we are not told who owns or rents this property, the size of the room suggests a locale in a wealthy area, for soon, about 120 believers occupied it. Most likely, it is in this same room where the community gathered to await the coming of the Spirit in Acts 2:1-4, as they would do on other occasions for teaching, preaching, and worship services (cf. Acts 4:31).

Acts 9:36-41 depicts another wealthy residence. This time it is located in Joppa, which is a long way from Jerusalem. Its owner, Tabitha, is a generous woman of means. Her description as a woman "full of good works and acts of charity" (9:36) tells us this. When she dies, she is laid out in the upper room, which is the biggest and best room in her house (9:39). This is so all the widows and the poor who have benefited from her charity can pay their respects. Surely, the community had gathered in this room many times before her "death." Just as surely, it was in this same room that they celebrated her return to life when, after Peter touched her, "she sat up" (9:40).

Acts 12:12-17 describes a third home. This one belongs to Mary, the mother of John Mark. Believers are again in a room that is large enough to hold them, for "many [*kanoi*; implying a considerable number of people; cf. Acts 14:21; 19:19; and 1 Cor 11:30] were gathered together and were praying" (12:12). Mary's home even had a courtyard that was attended at night by a servant named Rhoda (12:13), and it was secured (12:16). As such, it served as a buffer between the street, the courtyard, and the rooms in the house. What's more, it must have been used as one of the regular meeting places of the Jerusalem Jesus believers since Peter, upon his miraculous release from Herod's prison, knew where to find the group (12:12).

In sum, it appears early Judean Jesus followers in Palestine met in both humble and less than humble locales. They also met in more homes than the few places Luke references, for he reports that the church grew rapidly (cf. Acts 2:41, 47; 4:4; 5:14; 6:7). Wherever they met, they shared teaching, fellowship, the breaking of bread, and prayer (Acts 2:42), which is something they could never have done in the temple or in synagogues.

Greco-Roman housing. Most early Jesus believers we meet in the New Testament met in houses of a Greco-Roman design, for they were either in cities like Rome or in romanized centers on major trade routes throughout western Asia Minor and in places that would later be known as Greece. These buildings were of a different sort. Ninety-seven percent of Rome's population, for example, lived in *tabernae* (houses with shops) or in *insulae*, which were large, multiunit housing complexes that often occupied an entire city block.[10] Remains at Pompeii, Herculaneum, and Ostia show evidence of these dwellings.

It is thought *insulae* originated in Rome to address the city's growing housing needs. Similar to modern-day apartment houses, most *insulae* rose four to five stories high, and its tenants were from different socioeconomic classes. *Insulae*:

> were typically built around an inner courtyard that provided light and air to the rooms above. Small shops (*tabernae*) were often built into the outer ring of the first floor of the *insula*. Families who operated such small shops lived in them as well. There was sometimes a back room behind or a mezzanine above the main room, offering a bit of privacy for the family. A few "deluxe" apartments might be found behind these shops, facing the inner courtyard. These apartments contained a number of rooms, including accommodations for servants, and were suitable for hosting small social gatherings.[11]

Humbler apartments above the ground level were quite small. Truly, the higher up one lived, the smaller the rooms were (some down to thirty or thirty-five square feet), while the number of people living in them increased. Like the poorer homes in Palestine, very few people could meet in them since, more often than not, the same room served as the family's sleeping chamber, kitchen, and socializing area. Meetings in *insulae* cannot be ruled out entirely though, such as the House at Troas where a boy fell out of a third story window while listening to Paul attests (cf. Acts 20:9), but their use would have been rare. Besides, most *insulae* contained neither kitchen nor latrine facilities and were too small to be considered as places to meet with friends. Accordingly, their residents would have done their eating, drinking, and socializing outside.[12]

In contrast, 3 percent of Rome's population lived in a *domus*-type dwelling, which was an aristocratic Roman house. In addition to private rooms and offices for the owner, as well as quarters for the family and slaves,[13] these houses possessed an *atrium* (an inside central courtyard) and a *triclinium* (dining room), which with some rearranging could comfortably accommodate thirty-five to fifty people. Aristocratic houses that have been excavated in Pompeii, Ephesus, and Corinth give us a good idea of their space.[14] Excavations at Pompeii and Herculaneum also reveal that *domus*-type dwellings existed alongside *tabernae* and *insulae*.

Once again we see that the early Jesus believers gathered in groups in what was available to them, their homes. Small groups met in one another's homes or in their workshop-residences (as we have already seen with Priscilla and Aquila in Corinth), while the "whole" community gathered in larger setups to celebrate the Lord's Supper (cf. 1 Cor 11:17-34). Such gatherings would occur in the houses of the well-to-do or, perhaps, in rented first-floor "deluxe" apartments of the *insulae*, since their physical structures were conducive to larger groups. The hospitality of a host's dining area (*triclinium*) in particular, which reflected Jesus' own choice of an upper room for his last supper, his own choice of "non-sacred space" as the environment of his work, and his insistence on familial ties among the believers, was an especially cherished space (see 1 Cor. 11:18-22).[15] Cherished too was the security, intimacy, and privacy that houses (rarely *insulae*) could afford, all of which were important elements for an effective house gathering.

(2) Special Attention to Family Relationships and Terminology

The center of Greco-Roman society was the household (*oikos* or *oikia*). The center of the early Jesus groups was also the household. One built upon the other. This is a significant point because by New Testament times the household was regarded as the basic political unit that encompassed one's immediate and extended family. It was both a patriarchal institution and a "state" within the "state." The *kyrios/paterfamilias* (senior male of the family) had absolute power and authority, and he acted on behalf of the household. Slaves, freedmen, servants, day workers, tenants, business clients, and even household gods (who solidified the members of the household with each other and the household with Roman society) were part of his *oikos/familia*. Indeed, household loyalty was so strong, Augustus introduced the concept of the empire as a household writ large with himself as its *paterfamilias*. As such, members of the household were expected to worship his *genius* (i.e., his generative and protective spirit), thereby giving honor to the head of the empire's household. Early Jesus followers could not exist in such a milieu without some of its environment leaving its mark on them. In their case, they took what was best and challenged the rest, in whatever ways that they could, since they belonged to the household of God (cf. 1 Tim 3:15).

Households in the Greco-Roman world.[16] Much about the ancient household was repressive. Men ruled; women, children, and slaves obeyed; and everyone had and knew their place. Legal and moral codes of conduct spelled out how the *paterfamilias* should rule his household for the benefit of the community. Codes and traditions also indicated how wives, children, or slaves should act toward their husbands, fathers, or masters, respectively. One example of the "codes" comes from the Hellenistic discussion "concerning household management" (*peri oikonomias*), outlined by Aristotle in *Politics* 1.1253b.1-14.[17] A thumbnail description of the place of wives, children, and slaves in society follows.

Women were expected to run the household and be dignified, chaste wives and good mothers. They were the nurturing and binding element in the family, but they were always cast in a supportive role to men. Women's activities were limited, although by the period of the New Testament a "new woman" had begun to emerge. Women's lives also varied greatly, based on their position in society. *Laudatio Turiae*, a funerary inscription dating from the last decade of the first century BCE, is a window into what society's expectations of a wife were.[18] Plutarch's *Advice to the Bride and Groom*, which was written almost a century later, gives us another entry point.[19]

A child's life depended on the whim of his or her father. After birth, the baby was put at its father's feet. If he raised the child in his arms, it became part of the family. If he did not, it was removed from the house. For a long time afterward, children were seen by their mothers and tutors. From them, they were trained to obey their parents and be good citizens. Slaves, in particular, had no identity outside their family of ownership and could be acquired like any other form of property, that is, by inheritance, gift, or purchase. Slaves had no rights and were often used as objects and not as persons. Indeed, they could be bought and sold without question. Like children, slaves lived at the whim of their masters. In all instances, wives, children, and slaves were subordinates who lived under the authority of the master. Based on the example of Jesus, his early followers had other ideas, and many women and slaves were attracted to his liberating message.

Use of family language in the household of God. Belonging to Christ was not a personal affair; it had social dimensions. Believers entered into a community that Paul refers to as an *ekklēsia*, that is, to an assembly gathered together in faith. It is a term he employs more than sixty times in his letters, e.g., 1 Thessalonians 1:1. Since God was their father (1 Thess 1:1, 3; 3:11, 13), believers called one another "brothers" and "sisters," for they were members of a common household or family of faith (Gal 4: 5-7; 6:10; Rom 8:15-16; Eph 2:19; 3:14-15; 5:1; 6:23). Today, we would call them "fictive kin," for Jesus believers gave one another a kinship title and treated each other as if they had the actual kinship relationship implied by the name.

Adelphos (brother/sister) is Paul's favorite way of referring to the members of the communities to whom he wrote. It is also how he refers to his coworkers (cf. Gal 1:2; 1 Cor 1:1; 16:20; 2 Cor 1:1; 2:13; 8:23; 9:3, 5; Phil 2:25). Paul draws on this gender-inclusive term 114 times, with the same range of meanings the word "folks" has today in American English. Moreover, as *adelphos* expresses the basic relationship and attitude that should exist among all the believers in the household, master through slave, Paul expects Jesus-group members to behave in an *adelphos* way (cf. 1 Cor 8:11, 13; Rom 14:10-15). Paul's letter to Philemon is an example. For here it appears Paul expected the master-slave relationship between Philemon and Onesimus to be changed into an *adelphos* relationship, given Onesimus' new identity (cf. Phlm 16).[20] Moreover, because houses created a "family" atmosphere, it was possible for the believers, like Philemon, to practice *adelphos* love in personal and concrete ways.

Paul uses other familial terms in his writings. He describes his own work as that of a "father" (1 Thess 2:11; 1 Cor 4:14-15) or "mother" (Gal 4:19; 1 Thess 2:7, 11; 1 Cor 3:2), and he regards Onesimus as "my child . . . whose father I have become" (Phlm 10). He also reminds the Philippians of how "as a son with a father [Timothy] has served with me in the gospel" (Phil 2:22). Surely, we are in a more tender and welcoming house. If there is one message Paul enunciates in 1 Corinthians 11:17-34 it is this: that the *ethos* of the secular world (in this case Corinth) had no place at the table where the Lord presides. All were welcomed, for as Paul says elsewhere: "There is neither [Judean] nor Greek, there is neither slave nor free, there is neither male nor female; for you are all one in Christ Jesus" (Gal 3:28). In short, Jesus believers were siblings of one other, in one household, under the *paterfamilias of God*.[21]

For many reasons, early believers' behavior and thinking would put them at odds with everyone else. Women, for instance, could not attend meals with guests from outside the family, as Dio Cassius tells us (cf. *Roman History* 48.44.3; 55.2.4, 8.2; 57.12.5). For while Livia reclined with Octavian (a.k.a. Augustus) at their wedding, at official banquets celebrating military triumphs and other public occasions, Augustus presided with the men, while she gave a separate banquet for the women. In fact, houses excavated in Pompeii show evidence of two dining rooms side by side: one for men and the other for women. Yet depictions in the catacombs show men and women believers of different social ranks "breaking bread" together. A banquet scene fresco from room 45 in the SS Marcellino and Pietro catacomb in Rome is an example. While this scene comes from the late third or early fourth centuries, it depicts family rituals that go back to the early believers' practice (cf. 1 Cor 11:17-34). Such a flagrant disregard of societal norms could not have gone unnoticed, since secular art from the same period has men and women eating separately.

New Testament household codes: Oppressive or liberating? Some scholars think that since the household was viewed as the primary institution through which order was kept in society, the later post-Pauline and Pastoral Letters included "household codes" to show the Romans that Jesus believers were compliant residents of the empire.[22] A close look at what these "codes" say, however, shows that while there might be some similarities with their Greco-Roman counterparts, there are also significant differences. Aspects of Ephesians 5:21–6:9 are an example.

At its start, the entire household, including the husband, is equally instructed to "be subject to [i.e., voluntarily place themselves at the disposition of] one another out of reverence for Christ" (v. 21). It is Jesus, and not the husband, who is the master of the house, and it is Jesus' self-giving love that becomes the model by which everyone in the house is to pattern their ways of relating to each other. Truly, loving his wife in the same manner Christ loves (v. 25) is the only rule husbands are given relative to how they are to govern "their" household. Moreover, husbands are also commanded in Ephesians 5:25, 28, and 33 to love their wives with an *agape* love, which puts a decisive end to the *eros* kind of relationships they had with unattached women as they had once been "privileged" to do in the wider society. Responsibility and mutual submission, rather than patriarchal oppression, were the hallmarks of a believing family's household. Felix Just, SJ, includes a careful study of four of the five New Testament "household codes" on his website (http:// catholic-resources.org/Bible/Epistles-HouseholdCodes.htm). First Timothy 2:8-15; 6:1-10 is not included. I am indebted to him for both his insights and the use of his chart. Notice which groups are addressed and in which verses in each letter, what they are told to do, and why.[23]

Col 3:18–4:1	Eph 5:21–6:9	Titus 2:1-10	1 Peter 2:18–3:7
[cf. 3:1-17 addressed to *all*: lists of vices and virtues]	[*all*]: be subject to one another out of reverence for Christ (5:21)	*you* (sg.): teach what is consistent with sound doctrine (2:1). Tell the [*following groups*] to . . .	[*all* of you: have unity of spirit, etc. (*at end*: 3:8-12)]
wives: "be subject to your husbands, as is fitting in the Lord" (3:18)	*wives*: be subject to your husbands, as you are to the Lord; etc. (5:22-24)	*older men*: be temperate, serious, prudent, sound in faith, love, etc. (2:2)	*wives*: accept husbands' authority; don't adorn yourselves outwardly (3:1-6)
husbands: love your wives and never treat them harshly (3:19)	*husbands*: love your wives, just as Christ loved the Church, etc. (5:25-33)	*older women*: be reverent, not slanderous, teach & encourage younger women (2:3-5)	*husbands*: be considerate of your wives, paying honor to them (3:7)
children: obey your parents in everything . . . your accept-able duty in the Lord (3:20)	*children*: obey your parents in the Lord, for this is right, etc. (6:1-3)	[*younger women*: love their husbands and children, be self-controlled (2:4-5)]	x
fathers: "do not provoke your children, or they may lose heart" (3:21)	*fathers*: do not provoke your children to anger; bring them up in the Lord (6:4)	*younger men*: be self-controlled, do good works, say nothing evil, etc. (2:6-8)	x
slaves: obey earthly masters in everything . . . fearing the Lord (3:22-25)	*slaves*: obey your earthly masters, as you obey Christ (6:5-8)	*slaves*: be submissive to their masters; don't talk back, be faithful, etc. (2:9-10)	*slaves*: accept masters' authority, even if you suffer; Christ also suffered (*at beginning*: 2:18-25)
masters: treat your slaves justly & fairly; you also have a Master in heaven (4:1)	*masters*: stop threatening your slaves; you have the same Master in heaven (6:9)	x	x

While these codes do not show the kind of "equality" modern society would have wanted for wives and slaves, which is something that wasn't even a possibility until the eighteenth century, their language prescribes a much greater degree of "mutuality" than we first thought.[24] In fact, given the time, place, and culture in which they were written, it appears *that where they could*, the authors of the letters in which these "codes" are found "pushed the envelope to its edge."[25] Indeed, in its own way, husbands seem to be given more directives here than they were in Plutarch! The theme of the entire section, therefore, is not that "wives should submit to their husbands" or that slavery should be sanctioned but that in the household of believers, attitudes of love and kindness rule.

(3) Several Households: "One Accord" vs. Party Strife?

As the Jesus groups in each local area grew in size, it became more difficult for all the believers to meet as one. Accordingly, they met in several places, and, it appears, they gathered according to common practices (cf. Acts 12:12). For here, Peter, newly released from prison, seeks out the place where "many" but not all the believers in Jerusalem were meeting. Then, after describing how the Lord delivered him, Peter requests that what he has just shared with the believers in the house of John Mark's mother be communicated "to James and to the brethren" who are in another place (Acts 12:17). Quite possibly it is in the "Upper Room" of Acts 1:13-14, as Filson suggests.[26] From this vignette scholars posit there were at least two organizational forms existing in the Jerusalem Jesus group by that time: Aramaic-speaking Judean Christ believers and Greek-speaking Hellenists. Some believers met with James and his brothers, while others met in the house of Mary, the mother of John Mark. As Mary's family was related to the Cypriot Barnabas (cf. Col 4:10), they were probably Greek-speaking Jesus followers. Each group's practices would not be the same, since Judean Christ believers vigorously kept the law of Moses. And we know, despite Luke's wanting us to think the early believers acted "with one accord" (cf. Acts 1:14; 2:1), that they did not always act in an *adelphos* kind of way.[27] "The Hellenists murmured against the Hebrews because their widows were neglected in the daily distribution [of food]" (Acts 6:1) is an example. A Judean Jesus group and a Greek-speaking Jesus group also exist in Antioch, between which Peter was found (Gal 2:11-13). Notice how Paul reacts.

Evidence of division occurs in the Pauline literature as well. Otherwise, there would be no need for Paul constantly to encourage his congregations to work toward unity, as he does, for example, with the Corinthian and Philippian believers. For, while he may greet "the [*ekklēsia*] of God which is at Corinth" (1 Cor 1:2; 2 Cor 1:1), we know "factions" (subgroups) existed within the group (cf. 1 Cor 1:11-13). Divisions here

> are based on some form of alleged patronage. Whatever the nature of this divisiveness, the Corinthian church is clearly showing the strain of diverse groups within it. The existence of house churches within the city-wide church would go a long way to explain how such groups could arise.[28]

Paul's call to unity in 1 Corinthians 1:10 sets the standard: "I appeal to you, [brothers and sisters], by the name of our Lord Jesus Christ, that all of you agree and that there be no dissensions among you, but that you be united in the same mind and the same judgment." Similarly, in the same chapter of Romans where he mentions different house churches, Paul urges the whole church "to take note of those who create dissensions and difficulties, in opposition to the doctrine which you have been taught" (Rom 16:17). Moreover, he underlines the importance of unity by addressing his letters to both the Roman and Corinthian communities to the whole *ekklēsia* in their locales. In so doing, he provides an additional reminder to these communities of the larger movement to which they belong. There are many reasons why converts to the Jesus movement would have had difficulty being one in the world of the first century. Filson's next point addresses one of them.

(4) Early Believers Were a Cross Section of Society

The early Jesus movement grew in a milieu of social stratification, yet it attracted believers from all levels of society. Nowhere is this more evident than in Corinth. For the believers here, however small (thirty-five to fifty people amid its four hundred thousand inhabitants), reflect the same diversity that exists in the city. While Paul tells us that not many of the assembly are "wise according to worldly standards, not many were powerful, not many were of noble birth" (1 Cor 1:26), a few members have social standing. Crispus is a synagogue ruler (Acts 18:8), and Erastus, it is supposed, was the city treasurer (Rom 16:23). Some members have enough money to engage in legal proceedings (1 Cor 6:1), while others, such as Gaius, Stephanus, and Priscilla and Aquila, provide meeting places for the believers in their homes. Indeed, nine of the seventeen names Paul mentions in his letter are middle class and above. Other congregants do not have social standing and have to work (1 Cor 11:22), and there are slaves and former slaves in the community (1 Cor 7:20-24), as well as some freeborn persons. While there are rich and poor among the Corinthian Jesus group, however, no one is poverty stricken, since Paul presumes they can all make some contribution to the collection for the poor in Jerusalem (1 Cor 16:2; 2 Cor 8:1-6).

Ethnically and religiously, the Corinthian converts are also a mix. Greek and Latin names are among those Paul mentions and he refers to circumcised believers in Corinth (1 Cor 7:18); at the same time he pleads against members of the community's participation in feasts in the city's temples (cf. chap. 10). Finally, there are some members who are married to unbelievers (1 Cor 7:12-16). Such a mix was bound to raise problems, and it is clear from the opening verses of Paul's letter that the Corinthian community's diverse social, ethnic, and religious origins have led to conflict and division. Likewise, individual expectations and perspectives, as well as old ways of doing things, have begun to conflict with the standards of Jesus. Nowhere was this situation more evident than when the community gathered for worship. Accordingly, Paul addresses the issue.

At stake are past expectations, for according to Roman Corinthian table ethics, people of status ate more, ate better, and ate first. Likewise, since guests of higher status ate with the host in the *triclinium*, the owner of the house where the community gathered (here, perhaps at Gaius') invited his friends to come earlier. Obviously they ate and drank to excess (1 Cor 11:21), to the degree that when the poorer members of the community arrived late because they had to work, little remained for them. Upon hearing about this, Paul explodes and decries all the behaviors he deemed inappropriate among those celebrating the Lord's Supper (1 Cor 11:17-22). For while protocols of privilege were expected at secular tables in Corinth, such conduct was a violation of their unity and unacceptable at a table where the Lord presides. In sharp contrast he then re-presents the tradition of the Lord's Supper as a critique of their behavior and as a basis of his corrections of their excesses (1 Cor 11:23-25).

The list of believers Paul mentions in Romans 16:3-16 also includes a mixture of people with varying ethnic, religious, and social backgrounds.[29] Twelve of twenty-six believers he mentions are greeted by Paul in a way that seems to indicate he knows them personally. Perhaps some of the Judean Jesus followers, like Priscilla and Aquila, had settled in Corinth after being expelled from Rome in 49 CE, and, like the couple, they returned to Rome after Claudius' death in 54 CE.[30] Some of them may have even gathered for prayer and fellowship in Priscilla and Aquila's home in Corinth, before and after Paul arrived there. In fact, at least one of the people Paul greets, Epaenetus, was part of their house church in Ephesus, and as "the first convert in Asia" (Rom 16:5b), he was probably instructed by them.

While Paul seems to know that five house churches exist in Rome, he knows only a few of their members personally. No doubt he heard about the others through Priscilla and Aquila. One group meets in their house (16:5a). Others belong to the households of Aristobulus (16:10b) and Narcissus (16:11b), neither of whom appear to be Jesus followers, and there are two further groups that include Asyncritus, Phlegon, Hermes,

Patrobas, and Hermas (16:14) and Philologus, Julia, Olympas, and Nereus and his sister (16:15). Thus:

> While the majority of members were probably drawn from the lower class, predominantly slaves or freed persons (*libertini*), some at least were of sufficient means to have houses large enough to accommodate gatherings of the separate *ekklēsiai*. But the numbers of persons of higher social standing was probably very small. Composed largely of persons not born in Rome, the community spoke Greek.[31]

Once again, we are in the presence of a mixed group of people who would never have come together under other circumstances. The fact there is no evidence for either a central coordinator or a worship facility in Rome at that time indicates they did not.[32] Nor did they until well into the second century, as Justin Martyr (*First Apology* 67) remarks. So, like the early believers did in Jerusalem, Roman Jesus followers met in privately owned locations and with others that held the same religious beliefs and practices. That they did so helps to explain the tensions between "the strong" (Hellenist Jesus followers who emphasize their freedom from the Torah) and "the weak" (Judean Jesus followers who observe the Judean holy days and dietary practices) that Paul attempts to bring together in Romans 14:1–15:13. Truly, if there is one impression Paul's greetings in Romans 16:3-16 conveys it is that there are a number of Jesus groups in Rome that are not in relationship to one another. Accordingly, one of the purposes of his greetings may have been to reinforce a sense of unity.[33]

(5) WOMEN EMERGE AS LEADERS IN THE HOUSE CHURCH

In all probability, the "owners" as innate leaders of the houses the earliest believers met in would have provided the leadership of the meeting, since they were the "patrons" of the assembly. In truth, house church settings had a significant impact on women's leadership opportunities. In Corinth, for example, Prisc(ill)a and Aquila, Gaius, and perhaps Stephanus, Chloe, and Phoebe were both hosts and leaders of the Jesus groups that met in their homes. This same principle would be true in Rome. Prisc(ill)a and Aquila are the prime example. In fact, early on Paul was free enough to acknowledge this couple's leadership when he left them "in charge" in Ephesus (Acts 18:21). In looking at the list of people Paul greets in Rome, it is also obvious that women were equal to men as leaders in the nascent assemblies. House leadership in other areas tell the same tale, as memories of Mary of Jerusalem, Lydia of Philippi, and Dorcas of Joppa evidence.

In Sum: What a New Testament House Church Is

If anyone asked for directions to a "church" in the first century, they would have been directed either to a private home or to a rented space, as it was in domestic dwellings that the "family of God" gathered together as *ekklēsia* to study, pray, and worship in small groups. Occasionally, these smaller "cells" joined together as a larger group. Household terminology informed their practice, for Jesus followers considered themselves as brothers and sisters under the same father, God. As such, all the traditional categories collapsed. Instead, Judean and Greek-speaking believers were *adelphos*. Consequently, masters were to step down to the same level as their "brother" and "sister" slaves, and males were to recognize that females were both their "sisters" and equals (cf. Gal 3:28). Hopefully, there were more successes than failures in this regard. Some groups, however, tended to meet along party lines, which house churches in Jerusalem, Corinth, and Rome evidence. From this we see that reality vis-à-vis challenges were a part of the picture from the very start. Returning to 1 Corinthians 16:19 we will now imagine what the church that meets in the house of Aquila and Priscilla does.

What a House Church Does

Everyone delights in hearing from their friends; the Corinthian Jesus groups would have as well. They would have especially appreciated the warmth and support the Ephesian Jesus group's greetings conveyed. Most important, they would have reveled in the greetings that came from the believers who met in the home of Aquila and Prisc(ill)a, which included Paul. In receiving these greetings, Corinthian believers would also have been reminded of some of the wonderful moments they had shared in this couple's home. Indeed, in its own way, 1 Corinthians 16:19 provides a window into the first component of what a house church does. For, *house churches provided a space where believers could gather together, thanks to the hospitality of a host, to be both strengthened and supported by each other*. It is what *koinōnia* (i.e., the close connection or relationship among community members, their mutual support of one another, and the empathy and participation in each other's lives) was all about![34] Whereas, gods and goddesses appear to ask their adherents "What have YOU done for ME today?" as a test of their fidelity, Jesus believers were asked to live their faith by loving each other as Jesus had loved them (cf. John 13:12-15). House churches gave them the space to grow in that love.

Acts 2:42 provides a thumbnail sketch of what house church meetings included, for in the private and familial space hosts and leaders provided, believers "devoted themselves to the apostles' teaching . . . to the breaking of bread [the Eucharist or the Lord's Supper as it is variously called][35] and the prayers." Accordingly, *house churches provided a space where believers could also be nourished by the Word and by Eucharist*.

Prisc(ill)a and Aquila are quintessential house church hosts. Up to this point, we have learned a few things about their hospitality. First, we have seen how they made their home available as a meeting place for other believers to share their faith. Indeed, they probably did this in Rome before they were expelled in 49 CE and then again in Corinth before and after Paul arrived there. Later, they welcomed Paul, an itinerant missionary, to live with them, and perhaps even Timothy and Silas when they arrived in Corinth from Macedonia (cf. 2 Cor 11:9). Next they engaged in a missionary outreach, leaving everything behind to accompany Paul to spread the good news about Jesus in Ephesus. He even left them there as his advance team when he went on to Antioch, Galatia, and Phrygia (Acts 18:21-23). First Corinthians 16:19 shows they opened their home to yet another fledgling group.

Other texts give us some idea of the range of activities that went on in their house. Acts 18:24-26, for example, tells us that Priscilla and Aquila taught. More than likely, this teaching took place in their home. That Priscilla's name appears first in the text (at a time when rank mattered) seems to indicate she was Apollos' main tutor. Bonnie Thurston enunciates what teaching implied: *kērygma*, i.e., preaching or proclamation to those not yet followers of Jesus with the intent of bringing them to belief, and *didachē*, or teaching those already converted with the intent of deepening their understanding of what commitment to Jesus meant.[36] Surely, in Apollos' regard, Priscilla and Aquila were involved in *didachē.* That they succeeded in their teaching is evidenced by his reception in Corinth. They were also involved in *kērygma*. Most likely, Epaenetus was among the first of their students (Rom 16:5b).

Without a doubt, Prisc(ill)a and Aquila also shared their faith, read and prayed from the Septuagint (the Greek Old Testament), and passed on to the Ephesian and later Roman Jesus believers what they had learned from Paul. As people who had already demonstrated their living faith in Jesus as the Messiah of God (cf. Acts 18:2), they had much to share. In addition, they would have provided the space for the celebration of the Eucharist, and since the Lord's Supper was still celebrated within the context of a full meal, as patrons, they would have supplemented what the community brought. Likewise, they would have led prayer services, which, according to 1 Corinthians 14:26, would have included hymns, lessons, and interpretations. Finally, as host and leaders they would have been responsible to "build up the body" by maintaining order. For it appears Paul was disappointed that the later leaders in Corinth hadn't maintained the necessary order of the Lord's Supper (1 Cor 11), nor were they functioning as arbitrators of disputes among the brethren (1 Cor 6) or maintaining a moral discipline (1 Cor 5).[37] We will now turn to Romans

16:3-5 to see what these verses can add to the picture of Prisc(ill)a and Aquila as house church leaders and hosts.

Romans 16:3-5

Greet Prisca and Aquila, my [coworkers] in Christ Jesus, who risked their necks for my life, to whom not only I but also all the churches of the Gentiles give thanks; greet also the church in their house.

Chapter 16 vis-à-vis Paul's Letter to the Romans

Paul's greetings lie in the final chapter of his letter to the Romans, but until recently, many scholars debated whether they belonged there. Thinking Paul could never have known so many people in a community he neither founded nor visited, New Testament interpreters concluded these verses were later added to it. Textual evidence for the existence of a shorter edition of Romans (in one case, chaps. 1–14, and in another, chaps. 1–15) supported their claim. Accordingly, it was suggested that Paul's greetings were part of a letter to the Ephesian community that was mistakenly included in the editing of Romans. Today, however, thanks to the work done by H. Gamble (*The Textual History of the Letter to the Romans* [Grand Rapids, MI: Eerdmans, 1977]), many scholars have changed their mind. Indeed, they not only think Paul's concluding thoughts are integral to the rest of his letter but that they also shed light on the composition and structure of the early church.[38]

Having said this, it becomes clear that some time before Paul wrote his letter to the Romans, which most scholars date to around 57 CE, Prisc(ill)a and Aquila had returned to Rome. Claudius' death in the fall of 54 CE, along with the lapse of his edict, opened the door. Other Judean Christ believers returned "home" as well, some of whom Paul probably met in Corinth and Ephesus. Realistically, their arrivals would have had to have happened a year or so before Paul wrote his letter since there had to have been enough time for the situation he addressed in chapter 14:1–15:13 to have occurred.

While Paul recognizes twenty-six people in his personal greetings (twenty-four by name, plus two who are related to a named person), he places Prisc(ill)a and Aquila's names first, in the emphatic position. This is because in this instance they are his most important colleagues. In fact, he probably sent them back to Rome to act as his "advance team" as he had previously sent them ahead to Ephesus (Acts 18:18-21, 24-26; 19:1). In honoring this missionary couple, Paul stresses four things about them: (1) he regards them as his coworkers (*sunergoi*) in Christ Jesus; (2) they remained faithful to him (and by extension, to the gospel) to the point of "risk[ing] their necks [in some way] for my life"; (3) as such, everyone should appreciate their witness; and (4) believers are meeting in their home (cf. 1 Cor 16:19).

(1) My Coworkers in Christ Jesus

Paul uses the term "coworker" (*sunergoi*) when he refers to his colleagues. Urbanus (Rom 16:9), Apollos (1 Cor 3:9), Titus (2 Cor 8:23), Epaphroditus (Phil 2:25), Timothy (1 Thess 3:2; Rom 16:21), and Euodia and Syntyche (Phil 4:2-3) are a few examples. It is his favorite way to describe someone who works with him (and for and with God; cf. 1 Cor 3:9a) in proclaiming the gospel. In fact, all but one of the thirteen uses of this term in the New Testament occur in his writings. Verse 8 in 3 John is the sole exception. Indeed, words like *kopiaō/kopos* (to labor/toil) and *ergazomai* (to work) display Paul's understanding of ministry. It is a burden-bearing, suffering service for the gospel that he and his coworkers are willing to shoulder.[39] As such, 1 Corinthians 16:16-18 also makes clear that when Paul uses the term "coworker" he is talking about a leadership position, for here the Corinthians are urged to be subject to them. Notice, in acknowledging Prisc(ill)a and Aquila as his "coworkers" (Rom 16:3), Paul mentions Prisc(ill)a first! Equally important is the fact that he regards this couple as his "coworkers" even when he is absent from their ministerial endeavors, nor are they dependent on him for their role or position.[40]

(2) Faithful to the Point of Risking Their Necks for His Life

When Paul speaks about how Prisc(ill)a and Aquila "risked their necks" to the point of death, most commentators assume he is referring to his time in Ephesus and to the situation he references in 1 Corinthians 15:32a: "What do I gain if, humanly speaking, I fought with beasts at Ephesus?" Are the beasts animals? This is hardly the case since Paul lived to talk about it; nor did he include "fighting beasts" in his list of hardships in 2 Corinthians 6:5 and 11:23. Instead, he is using a standard metaphor in Hellenistic moral teaching. Here it refers to the "many adversaries" he has encountered, such as the ones he mentions in 1 Corinthians 16:9. And surely we know through Luke that there were men, such as the silversmiths, who acted like beasts in regard to him (cf. Acts 19:23-31). In any case, people such as these present Paul with situations (beasts) where he had to fight for his life (cf. 2 Cor 1:8-10). Obviously, on one such occasion, Prisc(ill)a and Aquila "risked their necks" for him (and for the gospel). It is a metaphor that means that they stood by him (and for God) when their own lives were put at risk.

(3) All the Churches of the Gentiles Should Share Paul's Appreciation[41]

That Paul expresses his gratitude for Prisc(ill)a and Aquila's service is understandable, but that he claims everyone else should be grateful to them baffles scholars. Even more, they puzzle over the oddity of non-Judean believers being asked to praise a Judean Christ-believing couple, and especially when they are part of a community that appears to be so divided (cf. Rom 14:1–15:13).[42] Perhaps the importance of unity is also Paul's point; for in praising them, he covertly underlines what he said in Romans 15:26-27 ("For Macedonia and Achaia have been pleased to make some contribution for the poor among the saints at Jerusalem; they were pleased to do it, and indeed they are in debt to them, for if the Gentiles have come to share in their spiritual blessings, they ought also to be of service to them in material blessings").

In each instance, Paul uses a positive example to encourage unity. For example, Prisc(ill)a and Aquila have moved so many times for the sake of the mission, they had probably suffered financial setbacks, which is another form of risking their necks. Because of their generosity, non-Judean Christ believers in Rome, Corinth, and Ephesus have benefited spiritually. Macedonian and Achaian Christ believers have also been generous. In their case, the financially strapped Jerusalem Judean Christ believers benefited. Indeed, Paul says the Macedonian and Achaian Christ believers were willing to financially aid the Jerusalem Judean Christ believers because they knew they had shared in their spiritual blessings (Rom 15:27). In each instance, because of believers' generosity, both Judean and non-Judean Christ believers (i.e., the whole *ekklēsia*) have profited. Robert Jewett is probably right when he suggests that the effusiveness of Paul's claiming gratefulness on the part of "all" the non-Judean Christians constitutes an implicit invitation for the Roman house churches to provide similarly audacious and perhaps risky aid to the Pauline mission just as Prisc(ill)a and Aquila had. In so doing, they may also become recipients of the universal thanks and praise of others.[43]

B. The Testimony of Deutero-Paul: 2 Timothy 4:19

Prisc(ill)a and Aquila's influence in the nascent Jesus groups was so great that they were included in the greetings of what some people regard as Paul's last letter. Most contemporary scholars, however, believe that the First and Second Letters to Timothy and the Letter to Titus were written long after Paul died, probably sometime between the late first century to the middle of the second century CE, and that they were written in

Paul's name by an unknown author or authors, and *were meant to inspire a general audience.*[44] Since the eighteenth century, these three letters are collectively referred to as the Pastoral Letters. This is because they were addressed to two individuals in their capacity as pastors and were concerned with how to shepherd the community and keep the faith.

In 2 Timothy, Paul writes to his "beloved child" Timothy (1:2) from prison (1:16-17; 2:9; perhaps the one reported by Acts 28:30), hoping he will remain as faithful a witness to the gospel as he himself has been, despite suffering and persecution (1:8-14; 2:1-13; etc.). Indeed, it is believed its author modeled this letter on Paul's real letter to the Philippians. Throughout the letter, Paul presents a picture of himself as *abandoned* ("You are aware, that all who are in Asia turned away from me, and among them Phygelus and Hermogenes" [1:15]); *harmed* ("Alexander the coppersmith did me great harm" [4:14]); and *deserted* ("For Demas, in love with this present world, has deserted me and gone to Thessalonica; Crescens has gone to Galatia, Titus to Dalmatia" [4:10]; also, "At my first defense no one took my part; all deserted me" [4:16]). Yet he remains faithful ("But the Lord stood by me and gave me strength to proclaim the message fully, that all the Gentiles might hear it" [4:17]). Such a depiction makes the names this author lists as those Paul greets, and who obviously are still faithful to him and the mission, all the more noteworthy. Indeed, they are part of the strength the Lord gave him. Prisc(ill)a and Aquila head the list.[45]

John Chrysostom also mentions Priscilla and Aquila in Homily 10 on Second Timothy (cf. 2 Tim 4:9-13). Of course at this point he, as did the vast majority of the early church fathers, thought that Paul had actually written the letter. In commentary on verse 19 he says:

> Salute Priscilla and Aquila, These are they of whom Paul makes continual mention, with whom too he had lodged, and who had taken Apollos to them. He names the woman first, as being I suppose more zealous, and more faithful, for she had then received Apollos; or it might be done indif-

ferently. And it was to them no slight consolation to be thus
saluted. It conveyed a demonstration of esteem and love,
and a participation in much grace. For the bare salutation
of that holy and blessed man was sufficient to fill with grace
him who received it.[46]

Like the unknown author of 2 Timothy, Chrysostom extols the
fidelity and pastoral sense of these two loyal collaborators of
Paul.

Summation: Prisc(ill)a and Aquila's Impact on the Nascent Jesus Groups according to Paul and Deutero-Paul

Without a doubt Paul valued Prisc(ill)a and Aquila, and he
commended them in a public way. He regarded this missionary
couple as his coworkers in Christ (Rom 16:3), and he knew they
were as committed to Jesus and to the gospel as he was. As such,
Paul took them to Ephesus when he left Corinth (Acts 18:18-19);
and he included their greetings, naming them first, when he
wrote to the Corinthians (1 Cor 16:19). Surely the very mention
of their names would have strengthened the Corinthians' faith,
since they would have remembered the part this couple had
played in the formation of their faith. Truly, some of them were
probably part of the community that met in their house.

Afterward, Paul sent this couple back to Rome as his advance
team before he would arrive there himself. Once again they
established a house church (Rom 16:5) that provided a space
where believers could gather to study, pray, and worship in a
small group and where they would be encouraged and nurtured
by the Word, each other, and the Eucharist. Indeed, Paul com-
mends their loyalty to the point that they "risked their necks"
for him (Rom 16:4) and by extension for the gospel.

Later, Prisc(ill)a and Aquila are raised up by the writer of the
second Deutero-Pauline letter to Timothy, where they are depicted as faithfully ministering with Timothy in Ephesus, when

so many others have abandoned Paul (2 Tim 1:15; 4:9-10). "Paul" even sends warm greetings to them (2 Tim 4:19). That they are listed first testifies to the enormous regard early believers and, in particular, the author of this letter knew that Paul had for them, for Prisc(ill)a and Aquila were among his oldest and most loyal collaborators. From the beginning of their collaboration with him to its end, *they were a presence that strengthened.*

CHAPTER 3

From Snippets to a Composite Picture

While Luke and Paul give us different information about Priscilla and Aquila, in the end there is a great similarity in what they tell us. Paul never states, for example, that Prisc(ill)a and Aquila are married; nor does he mention that they lived in Rome before they came to Corinth or that they moved from Rome because they were expelled from there (cf. Acts 18:2). Neither does Paul say he lived and worked with them as tentmakers while he lived in Corinth (cf. Acts 18:3) or that after a year and a half he took them with him to Ephesus (cf. Acts 18:18-19), much less that they carried on the mission while he traveled on to Antioch, Galatia, and Phrygia (cf. Acts 18:21-23). And he never indicates that they taught Apollos (cf. Acts 18:26). Perhaps this is because Paul doesn't seem interested in details; instead, he addresses the big picture. What he does tell us, however, affirms some of Luke's information.

That Paul sends Prisc(ill)a and Aquila's greetings to the Corinthians from Ephesus (1 Cor 16:19) admits to the fact not only that this couple was in both cities but also that they were important to the believers who lived in them. Surely, the "warm greetings" they sent the Corinthians (which he lists first) must have been received by these believers with great eagerness, for, more than likely, several of them had gathered to pray, study, and worship in their home, just as the Ephesian believers were now doing. Moreover, that in some way Prisc(ill)a and Aquila had "risked their necks" for Paul's life (Rom 16:4) coheres with the picture of their being willing to proclaim "Jesus as the Messiah of God" in some of the synagogues at Rome. In fact, it was probably this action that caused Claudius to expel them along with the other Judeans and Judean Christ followers who had incited riots (cf. Suetonius, *Claudius*, 25.4).

Finally, both authors would concur that Prisc(ill)a and Aquila were coworkers (*sunergos*) with Paul and that they were intimately involved in the life and faith of the early believers in at least three different cities. Indeed, were Luke and Paul to coauthor an anthology of the early Jesus believers this couple's entry would read something like this: Prisc(ill)a and Aquila were traveling missionaries in leadership positions in the early Jesus groups who impacted the lives of Jesus believers in Corinth, Ephesus, and Rome. As coworkers with Paul, they worked tirelessly and at great personal sacrifice for the cause of Christ and in the "defense of the gospel."

More should and could be said about them, however, as in the Greco-Roman world in which they lived, this couple would have been regarded as people of superior excellence, or virtue (*arête*). Likewise, because they had lived their lives with the highest effectiveness, much good had resulted from the use of their gifts and abilities. For this reason, everyone would have considered them worthy of honor. It was the highest praise that anyone could have bestowed on them.[1] Indeed, early in the second century CE, Gaius Julius Aquila put a personification of *arête* on the façade of the library he built in Ephesus to honor his father, Gaius Julius Celsus Polemaeanus, who had once been the governor of the province of Asia. Underneath the statue, Greek and Latin letters publicly heralded this component of his father's character. There was no better way he could ever have acknowledged him.

To be acknowledged as persons of excellence (*arête*), Priscilla and Aquila's lives (as Celsus' had) would have had to have evidenced three characteristics: (1) their words and deeds cohered; (2) their outreach (benefaction) was to all; and (3) they were willing to suffer, i.e., to endure hardships on behalf of the people or causes they served. The term for such courageous action in the line of duty is *peristasis*.[2]

How this works is best seen in the famous inscription of Priene, in the province of Asia, which celebrates the birthday of Caesar Augustus and which dated to 9 BCE. Because the citizens living there were so taken with the life, words, and deeds of Augustus, and his impact on *all* "humanity," they wanted to honor him by using his birthday (September 23) as the day on which they would begin a new year. Accordingly, Paulus Fabius Maximus, the proconsul of Asia, wrote a letter on their behalf to ask the Provincial Assembly to pass a resolution "that put into writing all his *aretai* [evidences of superior excellence], so that their recognition of what redounds to the honor of Augustus might abide for all time."[3] It worked, and the decree that the Asian League sent them was inscribed on a stele in Greek and Latin and set up in the temple. We still hear about Augustus' excellence today.

Priscilla and Aquila achieved this same recognition. In their case, they were honored for all time by three different authors within the pages of the New Testament. Using the criteria for excellence, we will now examine the texts to see how they had earned this recognition.

(1) Priscilla and Aquila's Words and Deeds Cohere

If ever a sentence captures this couple, it is this one: Priscilla and Aquila walk the talk everywhere we meet them. Their entry into nascent Christian history sets the stage, since their devotion to God so permeated their lives that it led to their being expelled from Rome in 49 CE (Acts 18:2). From the beginning, this couple preached the good news of what God was doing for believers in the *Christos*/Messiah. They could no more keep silent about that than Paul could, and, like him, they were unafraid of the consequences. Frederick W. Danker asserts that the "formulation 'word and deed' is especially typical of accolades to Greek or Roman benefactors and finds expression in such formulae as '(distinguished) for word and deed' and 'saying and doing what is good.'"[4] In other words, the laudatory word-deed formulation emphasized that the person or persons so described lived their lives in keeping with their rhetoric.

Should a person or persons be lauded in a believing sense, then, as Priscilla and Aquila will, it would mean that what they said they believed would be evidenced by the way in which they lived their lives, which is exactly what Paul means when he lauds this couple in Rom 16:4. They walked the talk. For this reason, as he says, the whole civilized world should give thanks for Prisc(ill)a and Aquila and praise them for their work. John Chrysostom raises them even higher when he says in his First Homily on the Greeting to Priscilla and Aquila:

> Behold here a man and a woman, and they excelled in the work place and practiced a trade and demonstrated a more accurate spiritual insight to those living in monasteries. Whence is this evident? From those things which Paul said about them before, rather not from those things which he spoke before, but from those to which he next bore witness. For after he said "Greet Priscilla and Aquila," he added their qualification of worth. What sort is this? He does not say that they were rich or distinguished or well born. What then? "My fellow-laborers in the Lord." Nothing could equal this in a reckoning of excellence. Their worth is evident not only because of this but also because he stayed with them, not just one day, or two or three, but two entire years: in this their virtue can be seen.[5]

Obviously, Priscilla and Aquila's words and deeds cohered. As such, they were distinguished by different authors in the New Testament for their "words and deeds" and for "saying and doing what is good."

(2) Their Outreach Is to All

Priscilla and Aquila opened their home on a number of occasions, and in a number of places. Undoubtedly, they hosted other Judean Christ believers in Rome before Claudius expelled them, as these early believers would have needed the strength of each other's faith and witness in order to do the courageous kind of things they did in the synagogues. Later, they hosted not only Paul for the eighteen months he lived in Corinth but more than likely Timothy and Silas as well when these missionaries arrived in Corinth with a gift for Paul from the Macedonian believers (Acts 18:5; cf. 2 Cor 11:9). Perhaps they even instructed Apollos in their home (Acts 18:26).

Other Judean Christ followers may also have settled in Corinth when they were expelled from Rome in 49 CE. Surely they gathered in this couple's home for prayer and the Eucharist, as they had done in Rome before their expulsion. Others may have joined them before Paul arrived, and even more people after Paul settled in Corinth. And we know from Paul's letters that Prisc(ill)a and Aquila hosted churches in their home in both Ephesus (1 Cor 16:19) and Rome (Rom 16:3). Indeed, their door was always open, however crowded the space!

Likewise, this couple was not afraid to reach out and help other converts to the faith, as they did with Apollos when it became apparent to them that he had not been taught everything about Jesus (Acts 18:26). Indeed, they were confident enough in their own learning, that they took on this "eloquent man, well versed in the scriptures" (v. 24) and filled him in with what was missing from his instruction. That they took him aside (i.e., privately) and "expounded to him the way of God more accurately" (v. 26) gives us a window into the way Priscilla and Aquila reached out to others. They never demeaned them.

It is also important to note that when Luke tells us that Apollos spoke "boldly in the synagogue" (Acts 18:26a), it was probably the same synagogue Paul had preached in before he left Ephesus (Acts 18:19-21) and the one in which Priscilla and Aquila later heard him preach (v. 26b). From this vignette we see that these believers continued to go to the synagogue, for here they could keep reaching out to the Judeans that Paul had himself tried to reach. Epaenetus, whom Paul calls "the first convert in Asia for Christ," may be a case in point (Rom 16:5).

(3) They Were Willing to Suffer

Inscriptions from the past show us with what importance ancient people regarded this third component of excellence. About the year 48 BCE, for example, the people of Dionosypolis, a city near the Black Sea, praised a philanthropist named Akornion, for risking "life and limb in any crisis [*peristasis*] that developed."[6]

Notice how Paul's later praise of Priscilla and Aquila fits in here, for he said, they had "risked their necks" for him (cf. Rom 16:4).

Likewise, an otherwise unknown bureaucrat named Menas was praised because it is stated that "he spares no expense in rendering public service nor gives thought to any hazard [*kindynos*] that imperils his own interests when he leaves on embassies in behalf of the city."[7] Is this not reminiscent of the generosity of this couple and their willingness to take up stakes and move from city to city in behalf of the gospel? Moreover, gathering other believers in their home would have impinged upon their privacy, but it never seemed to bother them. Interestingly, in another place, Paul tells his Philippian friends that they should fill their minds with "whatever is true, whatever is honorable, whatever is just, whatever is pure, whatever is lovely, whatever is gracious, if there is any excellence [*arete*], if there is anything worthy of praise" (Phil 4:8). The example of people like Priscilla and Aquila comes to mind.

Summation

However little we hear about Priscilla and Aquila, we know from what Luke and Paul tell us that they both epitomized excellence. Indeed, their lives and the good they were able to accomplish for many people in Rome, Corinth, and Ephesus testify to the fact that their words and deeds cohered, their outreach was to all, and they were willing to suffer for Christ and for the gospel. In addressing the Thessalonians, Paul beseeches this community to "respect those who labor among you and are over you in the Lord and [we] admonish you, and to esteem them very highly in love because of their work" (1 Thess 5:12-13). Surely, were Paul to address us today, Priscilla and Aquila would be among the believers he would recommend we esteem highly because of their work. Priscilla and Aquila have earned his and our recognition for they were, and are, *a presence to strengthen*.

CHAPTER 4

Learnings for Today

Let us greet Priscilla and Aquila and learn from them, for there are many important lessons we can glean from their lives. Accordingly, we will examine the texts we have that relate to them. From these texts, we can see their relationship with God and how it impacted the way they related to each other, Paul, his other collaborators, and the early believers in Jesus in three important places: Corinth, Ephesus, and Rome.

Priscilla and Aquila vis-à-vis God

From the beginning, Priscilla and Aquila were willing to be used by God as is evidenced by their constantly being on the move for the cause of the gospel. Their home was as moveable as the tents they made to support themselves, as it appears that, in a very short amount of time, they relocated both their home and their trade at least three times. Lest we forget, in contemporary terms, we are talking about moving between Italy, Greece, and Turkey. In fact, in introducing this couple, Luke tells us they had recently moved to Corinth because they had been expelled from Rome (Acts 18:3). Upon investigation, we discovered that it was probably because they were preaching that Jesus was the Messiah of God in some of Rome's syna-gogues. Thus, it becomes apparent that Priscilla and Aquila burned with the love of God and with what God was doing for them through Jesus. It was a message that needed to be heard, and Priscilla and Aquila were unafraid to preach it. They trusted God implicitly and were willing to risk everything for their faith. Such was their commitment.

Priscilla and Aquila Strengthen Each Other

In the six times we meet Priscilla and Aquila in the New Tes-tament (cf. Acts 18:2-3, 18-19, 26; Rom 16:3-5; 1 Cor 16:19; 2 Tim 4:19), with the exception of Luke's notation of Aquila's origins, they are never mentioned apart from each other. Indeed, we hear their names in the same breath. In terms of discipleship, they are the best-known married couple in the New Testament. In-deed, Pope Benedict XVI lifted them up as "models of conjugal life" in one of his general audiences.

While ministering in three important cities in the Roman Em-pire (Corinth, Ephesus, and Rome), Priscilla and Aquila taught, hosted both house churches and missionaries in their home, led services, and were willing to suffer for their faith and for the gospel. It is probable that they succeeded in doing these things because they lived and acted as one. Surely, they must have en-couraged, supported, and challenged each other. They knew each other's gifts and strengths and made the most of them. Everyone benefited. Teaching Apollos is an example of their insight and the use of their different gifts (Acts 18:24-26). For although Luke tells us "when Priscilla and Aquila heard [Apollos], *they* took him and expounded to him the way of God more accurately" (v. 26; em-phasis added), from John Chrysostom onward, interpreters have thought that by placing her name before Aquila's, Luke suggested Priscilla was Apollos' main teacher (cf. John Chrysostom's First

Homily [see p. 25], trans. Kroeger, 18). This is not to say that Aquila did not have a hand in Apollos' catechesis, but that he understood his wife was more gifted in this area and was unthreatened by it.

Furthermore, there is no suggestion of subordination in Priscilla's relationship to Aquila, as Meinrad Craighead's illustration beautifully captures (see p. xv in the introduction). They are an example of true mutuality in relationship. Nor is there any hint of subordination in her relationship with Paul. Indeed, he refers to the *ekklēsia* in "their" and not "his" house in 1 Corinthians 16:19. In the male-dominated society of the Greco-Roman world, it is to Aquila and Paul's credit that they recognized Priscilla as their "equal." In fact, Paul called both Prisc(ill)a and Aquila his "coworkers in Christ Jesus" (Rom 16:3; my translation). It is a designation he used only to describe leaders in ministry, such as Timothy (1 Thess 3:2; Rom 16:21), Titus (2 Cor 8:23), Epaphroditus (Phil 2:25), and Euodia and Syntyche (Phil 4:2-3). Perhaps Paul, having lived with this couple and seeing firsthand the way they related to each other, had them in mind when he later composed his definition of love in 1 Corinthians 13:4-7. The Corinthians, to whom they sent "hearty [surely heartfelt] greetings" from Ephesus (cf. 1 Cor 16:19), would have also experienced their mutuality in their faith and conjugal life.

A reading from Proverbs 31:10-12 (NAB), which is usually read in relation to a wife, is appropriate, for in adapting it, this reading can easily refer to Priscilla and Aquila's life together:

> When one finds a worthy [spouse],
>   [their] value is far beyond pearls.
> [Husband and Wife], entrusting [their] heart[s] to [each other],
>   [have] an unfailing prize.
> [Both bring good to one another], and not evil,
>   all the days of [their lives].

By living similarly, Priscilla and Aquila's marriage was strong enough to survive the stresses they lived under that were the result of their moving, working, and ministering, to say nothing of the stress of being expelled by the emperor! Indeed, new life emanated from their marriage as they formed, nurtured, and sustained numerous believers in the various places they lived and ministered.

Priscilla and Aquila
Were a Presence that Strengthened

Priscilla and Aquila vis-à-vis Paul

Paul found a place in the home of Priscilla and Aquila when he first arrived in Corinth and within it were two kindred spirits. Their gifts of hospitality and companionship provided him with not only a base from which to evangelize but also a place where he could practice his trade. Most important, their friendship gave him the additional strength he needed to deal with the opposition he faced every Sabbath as a result of his "preaching [and] testifying to the [Judeans] that the Christ was Jesus" (cf. Acts 18:5). Undoubtedly, a passion for Christ and their faith in God united this trio. Priscilla and Aquila's loyalty, effectiveness, and support were so complete that Paul asked them to join him when he left Corinth for Ephesus (Acts 18:18).

Furthermore, because Paul trusted them, "he left them there" (v. 19) to continue doing what they had already done in Corinth while he traveled on to Antioch, Galatia, and Phrygia. Paul's trust in them was warranted, for while he was gone they taught (Acts 18:18-26), gathered believers in their home (1 Cor 16:9), and were likely responsible for Asia's first convert (Rom 16:15b). Later, he sent them back to Rome as his advance team. His subsequent greetings to the Roman believers testifies to how highly he regarded this couple (Rom 16:3-4). Their importance to him is also shown by the fact that they are the first people he recognizes in a list of twenty-six persons (v. 3). What is more, Paul raised this couple up as a model to the Roman community and he lauded their loyalty, for in some way they were willing to give their lives for him and for the gospel (v. 4a). That said, he further asserted that everyone should be grateful for the witness of their lives (v. 4b). Later, as Ivoni Richter Reimer asserts:

> If 2 Timothy can be understood to be a kind of "testament of Paul," it is a magnificent accolade to the missionary artisan couple, for they are handed over to the community, and as a result their memory is bound up with the memory of Paul.[1]

Priscilla and Aquila and the Early Believers

Exiled from Rome, Priscilla and Aquila knew the importance of being welcomed. Accordingly, they offered hospitality to the point of a fine art. Surely Paul felt at home during the eighteen months he lived with them in Corinth, and it is likely he lived with them again in Ephesus. Others, such as Timothy and Silas, may have also stayed in their home when they arrived in Corinth to see Paul (Acts 18:5).

The faith of believers was also formed and nurtured in their house. As Paul tells us, their home served as a meeting place for the early believers in both Ephesus (1 Cor 16:19) and Rome (Rom 16:3). Although neither Luke nor Paul say it, they probably hosted an *ekklēsia* in Corinth as well. In each case, Priscilla and Aquila opened their modest dwellings to the believers even though it was much less than the kind of space the Jesus believers gathered in at Corinth (cf. 1 Cor 11:17-34). For here, the Ephesian Jesus believers would have met in an all-purpose room above their shop. However cramped, believers in Rome, Corinth, and Ephesus found a space in Priscilla and Aquila's home where their faith in Jesus could grow.

The way in which this couple shepherded believers can be intuited from a vignette Luke includes in his narration in Acts. In it, he tells us that while attending a synagogue service, Priscilla and Aquila heard an eloquent speaker by the name of Apollos (cf. Acts 18:26). However powerful his words were, this couple knew from their own instructions (which assuredly included many nightly discussions with Paul) that what Apollos presented boldly was a defective version of the gospel, and they had the courage to say so. Moreover, they treated this earnest presenter with delicacy and respect. That after private instruction Apollos was able to be recommended as a preaching missionary to Corinth (Acts 18:27-28) and that Paul would consider him a coworker (1 Cor 3:9) emphasizes how much he grew in their company.

Lessons for Today

While there are many ways in which Priscilla and Aquila can serve as positive models for us today, for the sake of brevity we will offer only three of them here.

Priscilla and Aquila Are a Model for the Laity

Priscilla and Aquila showed the importance and place of lay leadership in the *ekklēsia* right from the start. Paul recognized he could never have done what he did in Corinth, Ephesus, or Rome without their help. Within the last thirty years, the church has come to see the importance of lay leadership as well. Concurrently, there has been a remarkable surge in lay participation in ecclesial ministry. Whereas in the past, pastoral positions were held mostly by priests and sisters, today that is not the case. Instead, as was reported in a 2005 publication:

> The number of lay parish ministers in paid positions on parish pastoral staffs (30,632) exceeds the number of priests in parish ministry. And the number of lay parish ministers continues to grow. Whereas 54 percent of parishes employed lay parish ministers in 1990, two-thirds of parishes employ them today. What was once a predominantly suburban phenomenon is now growing in every geographical locale, particularly in the inner city, urban business districts, and small towns. Lay parish ministers are a common and accepted presence in parishes across the country. This, indeed, is a development of revolutionary proportions.[2]

Since this publication in 2005 these numbers have continued to increase. The places where the laity can be found have also expanded. In truth, laymen and laywomen serve professionally in ecclesial ministry in more ways and in every diocese across the country on a full- and a part-time basis. They now head local church communities and serve as catechists, teachers, spiritual directors, bereavement councilors, diocesan chancellors, and youth and campus ministers. They minister to the sick in their homes and act as chaplains in hospitals. They lead worship services in the church and faith-sharing groups in their homes, and serve as directors of soup kitchens and shelters for the homeless. What is more, they are involved in many of the kinds of things Priscilla and Aquila would have done in the first century. Likewise, with fewer priests and the need to close and merge parishes, the laity's role in the life of the Christian community will expand even more. Since the Second Vatican Council, the U.S. Catholic bishops have recognized that the laity have also been called and gifted by God to take on an active and responsible part in the mission of the church (cf. U.S. Conference of Catholic Bishops statement [1980], followed by their pastoral letter "Called and Gifted for the Third Millennium" [1995]). Indeed, the bishops acknowledged the laity as their "Co-Workers in the Vineyard of the Lord" (November 2005). Paul would be pleased.

Many religious communities have also invited women and men to share in their charism and mission. Today, their associates can be found ministering everywhere in the continental United States and as missionaries in their foreign missions. Moreover, professional organizations, like the National Association for Lay Ministry, have been founded to support, educate, and advocate for lay ministers. These organizations also supply information for ongoing education and sponsor conferences, prayer days, and retreats so that lay ministers have the opportunities they need to go apart for reflective time and space. With families and multiple responsibilities to care for, married as well as divorced and single lay ministers have become aware that effective ministry is a balancing act that requires prayerful attention.

Priscilla and Aquila were movers and shakers among the various Jesus groups in the first century. As missionaries, teachers, collaborators of Paul and others, and patrons of house churches in three different cities, they helped people get where they wanted to go and obtain needed information, and they created spaces that offered vital infrastructure for the expansion and support of the movement, taking risks in the process.[3] Laywomen and laymen like Priscilla and Aquila continue to set out as movers and shakers in the twenty-first century:

> In the future, even more than at present, they will bring creative ministerial competence to setting up sites on the Internet, animating local communities through song and art, parish planning and administration, and evangelizing in countless other ways, both directly and indirectly.[4]

In short, laywomen and laymen will pioneer in uncharted ways today, as Priscilla and Aquila did in their own time, and they have a model couple that will inspire and strengthen them.

Priscilla and Aquila Are a Model for Team Ministry

While living in Ephesus, Paul wrote to his Corinthian friends in part to unify them and to make them aware of the importance and use of their gifts for the good of the whole community. In so doing, he used the metaphor of the body (1 Cor 12:4-31). Perhaps as he wrote he thought of his own experience of working with others. In this case, Priscilla and Aquila, whom he references in the same letter as his "coworkers in Christ Jesus" (Rom 16:3; my translation), would have been his most immediate examples.

Paul's metaphor can be used today in describing a team, defined by James and Evelyn Whitehead as a work group organized for interdependence.[5] In this instance, some members of the team would serve as "feet" or "hands" while others would be as "eyes," or "ears," or even a "nose" (cf. 1 Cor 12:14-21). They would all work together for good. Furthermore, since members of a team come together intentionally, they would be predisposed to augment each other's gifts for the good of the community. As, "If the whole body were an eye, where would be the hearing? If the whole body were an ear, where would be the sense of smell?" (v. 17). For while a staff may be organized to keep its members out of each other's way, teams intend to have their members get in each other's way.[6] Indeed, like the team of Priscilla and Aquila, today's teams have less sharply divided roles and will come to rely on one another's strengths and wisdom. It is a win-win situation.

We have already seen how Priscilla and Aquila lived their marriage as a team. They mutually shared authority and responsibility, and they valued and accepted each other's gifts. Likewise, there is no indication of a competition for power, but, rather, they complimented each other's efforts. They also made room for Paul. As such their married life and working life coalesced and it spilled over into the way they ministered. Indeed, their goals were so similar that whether they were physically present to each other or not, they were present to each other. Notice, for example, how Paul calls Prisc(ill)a and Aquila his "coworkers in Christ Jesus," even while he himself was in another city. He can do this because he knows that however far apart they are physically, they are of one heart when it comes to the mission.

Finally, as this artisan couple traveled to different locations and was involved with different cultures, ecclesial teams today will also be involved in a truly "world church." They are on a multicultural team. Indeed:

> Local parishes will involve a number of Asians, Pacific Islanders, Africans and Latin Americans, who will stand alongside North Americans and those of European roots as the constituents of a truly global family. Church members will be of all races and colors. Those whose skin is black, brown, yellow, red and white will stand next to one another in projects serving the poor, will sit beside one another doing research into the causes of poverty, will work

with one another in lay missions, and will sing and pray
with one another in eucharistic celebrations.[7]

Robert Maloney hopes that the multicultural character of twenty-
first-century Catholic parishes will be a clear witness to the unity
of the human race and that the gifts of various cultures will help
us to have a continually expanding vision.[8] It is the kind of hope
Paul had when he wrote Romans.[9] It must be the hope of us all.

Priscilla Teaches Us the Importance of Women's Equal Leadership

While both Luke and Paul highlight Priscilla's role in the nascent Jesus groups, others have attempted to reduce and mini-
mize her importance. Surely the Western Text (D) is a major
culprit, but there are others.[10] Indeed, Reimer contends, there
are no small and unimportant alterations of a text. All changes
contribute to the destruction of an image.[11] In Priscilla's case it
worked, for until 1900 and the work of Adolf von Harnack,
Priscilla's importance was suppressed. Today, however,

> the retrieval and accenting of the history of Priscilla as a
> story that attempts to preserve Priscilla as a fully rounded
> individual is important for women and men who can and
> will live their faith in their daily lives. Priscilla is owed
> "reparation" in the sense "that she is to be recalled again
> and again in memory in the fullness of her womanhood,
> as wife, tent-maker, highly valued co-worker of Paul and
> acquaintance of Apollos." But the retrieval is not simply
> for her sake. It should and can give others courage. It can
> encourage people who, just like Priscilla and Aquila, are
> risking their necks for others who are taking a stand against
> the terrifying power of sin, and, as a result are suffering
> repressive treatment at the hands of the powerful.[12]

Priscilla's witness, then, is an opportunity for us to "pass over"
into her story and to appropriate from it what we need for our-
selves today. Moreover, the question we should ask as we listen
to her story isn't, "Is every element of what we hear about

Priscilla's story true?" but rather, "What does God want me to learn from her story?" This is not to say that Aquila didn't have a prominent role to play in these texts as well, but that whatever they did was a mutual endeavor. Priscilla teaches us that!

Summation

The Word of God never tires. Such is the case with Priscilla and Aquila, for, after two thousand years, we can still learn from their example. First, because they were willing to be used by God, Priscilla and Aquila were effective ministers. Indeed, strengthened by God and each other, they were able to be present to Paul, his collaborators, and the early believers, even to the point of great inconvenience. Second, they accomplished their missionary work both within and outside of their home and marriage. They did this because they kept their eyes on the goal, making known what God was doing for us through Jesus. From that they learned how to balance. As such, others such as Paul and the early believers who met in their home could depend on them. Finally, they worked as a team, mutually supporting and affirming each other. Because of their ability to do these things, they were *a presence that strengthened*.

CONCLUSION

A Presence to Strengthen

Prisc(ill)a and Aquila epitomize the kind of person Seneca offered his friend Lucilius as an example to strengthen, protect, and inspire him (cf. *Ep* 11:8-10), for as Luke and Paul have shown us, they are people of exceptional character. As such, their example is useful. It was useful when Luke first introduced them, and it is useful today. Indeed, at a time when lay ecclesial participation in the church is on the rise, it is important to have a married working couple who do ministry as a guide, since "you can never straighten that which is crooked unless you use a ruler." Luke and Paul have given us both a guardian and an attendant. As such, it behooves each of us to:

> Cherish [Prisc(ill)a and Aquila for they are] of high character, and keep[them]ever before your eyes, living as if [they] were watching you, and ordering all your actions as if [they] beheld them. . . . [For] we can get rid of most sins, if we have a witness who stands near us when we are likely to go wrong. The soul should have someone whom it can respect,—one by whose authority it may make even its inner shrine more hallowed. Happy is the [person] who can make others better, not merely when he

75

[or she] is in their company, but even when he [or she] is in their thoughts! And happy also is [that person] who can so revere [another] as to calm and regulate [him- or herself] by calling him [or her]to mind! One who can so revere another, will soon be [him- or herself] worthy of reverence. . . . Choose a master whose life, conversation, and soul-expressing face have satisfied you; picture him [or her] always to yourself as your protector or your pattern. For we must indeed have someone according to whom we may regulate our characters; you can never straighten that which is crooked unless you use a ruler.[1]

NOTES

Introduction, pages xi–xviii

1. Ancient people believed in this principle as well. The Naxians, for example, placed a monster Sphinx high up on an ionic column outside the Temple of Apollo in Delphi to guard and protect it from evil; while others placed protecting Medusas on the roofs of special buildings, such as they did on the Library of Celsus and Hadrian's Temple in Ephesus.

2. Cited from Richard Mott Gummere, trans., *Moral Letters to Lucilius by Seneca*, vol. 1 (Cambridge, MA: Harvard University Press, 1917), 63–65. See also www.stoics.com.

3. Priscilla and Aquila are regarded as saints by several Christian churches. They are celebrated in the Roman Church on July 8, in the Greek Orthodox Church on February 13, and in the Lutheran Church with their pupil Apollos on February 13.

4. Some scholars claim that Acts reflects a distinctly antifeminist bias. William O. Walker, for example, avers in "The Portrayal of Aquila and Priscilla in Acts: The Question of Sources," *New Testament Studies* 54, no. 4 (2008), 490, that Luke changed "Prisca" to "Priscilla" as a way of belittling or disparaging Priscilla and thus downplaying her role as a leader in the Church. On the other hand, while she agrees that women have a limited role in the accomplishment of Luke's purposes in Acts, Gail R. O'Day ("Acts" in *Women's Bible Commentary*, ed. Carol A. Newsom and Sharon H. Ringe, exp. ed. [Louisville, KY: Westminster John Knox Press, 1998], 395) notes that Luke frames Acts around the ministries of Peter and especially Paul, because they embody for him the movement of the gospel from Jews to Gentiles. The ministries of all other teachers and leaders, male and female, are diminished as a result of this emphasis. It is important therefore to remember that Acts does not contain a representative picture of church

leadership. In addition, Luke's desire to present a picture of Christianity that would win favor in the Roman Empire led to a further diminishment of women's roles in Acts. Women were second-class citizens in the Roman Empire; public leadership roles were all held by men. (See "Everyday Life: Women in the Period of the N.T." in *Women's Bible Commentary*, 482–99). Luke shapes his treatment of women in Acts to conform to this Roman model." Ben Witherington III, "The Anti-Feminist Tendencies of the 'Western' Text in Acts," *Journal of Biblical Literature* 103, no. 1 (1984): 82, thinks the Western text (D) has an antifeminine bias as well.

5. Wayne A. Meeks, *The First Urban Christians: The Social World of the Apostle Paul* (New Haven, CT: Yale University Press, 1983), 59.

6. Harry J. Leon, *The Jews of Ancient Rome*, rev. ed. (Peabody, MA: Hendrickson, 1995), 75.

7. Robert Jewett, *Romans: A Commentary*, Hermeneia (Minneapolis: Fortress Press, 2007), 955, is an example. He claims Prisca's noble background is consistent with the ancient naming of the Santa Prisca parish in the Aventine district of Rome, which is probably on the site of the original house church that was named after her. The *Titulus Priscae* address also suggests that this expensive property was originally registered in Prisca's name and reverted to church ownership centuries later. The Catacomb of Priscilla, located in the country estate of the Acilian family, further confirms her noble origin. Elisabeth Schüssler Fiorenza, "Missionaries, Apostles, Coworkers: Romans 16 and the Reconstruction of Women's Early Christian History," *Word and World* 6, no. 4 (1986): 429, disagrees.

8. Jerome Murphy-O'Connor, "Prisca and Aquila: Traveling Tentmakers and Church Builders," *Bible Review* (December 1992): 42.

9. Ibid. Cf. I. Howard Marshall, *Acts*, TNTC, vol. 5 (Downers Grove, IL: IVP Academic, 1980), 309; Mary Ann Getty-Sullivan, *Women in the New Testament* (Collegeville, MN: Liturgical Press, 2001), 154; Ivoni Richter Reimer, "The Missionary Artisan Priscilla and the Universal Praise that Is Her Due (18:1-3, 18-19, 24-28)," in *Women in the Acts of the Apostles: A Feminist Liberation Perspective*, trans. Linda M. Maloney (Minneapolis: Fortress Press, 1995), 195.

10. Linda L. Belleville, "Women Leaders in the Bible," in *Discovering Biblical Equality: Complementarity without Hierarchy*, ed. Ronald W. Pierce and Rebecca Merrill Groothius (Downers Grove, IL: IVP Academic, 2005), 122.

11. Ibid., 122, n. 34. She also addressees Andreas Köstenberger's critique of her assertion in *JETS* 44 (2001): 36, which claims 1 Corinthians 16:19: "Aquila and Priscilla, together with the Church that meets in their house, greet you warmly" proves otherwise, by saying that here "their house" is a statement of ownership, not ministry, thus warranting the order.

12. See Ben Witherington III, *The Acts of the Apostles: A Socio-Rhetorical Commentary* (Grand Rapids, MI: Eerdmans, 1998), 539; and Beverly Roberts Gaventa, *Acts* (Nashville, TN: Abingdon Press, 2003), 255.

13. F. Scott Spencer, *Journeying Through Acts: A Literary-Cultural Reading* (Peabody, MA: Hendrickson, 2004), 188.

14. I found Craighead's image in Miriam Therese Winter, *WomanWord: A Feminist Lectionary and Psalter* (New York: Crossroads, 1991), 233, and I am using it with her gracious permission.

15. As Luke Timothy Johnson, *Acts of the Apostles*, Sacra Pagina 5 (Collegeville, MN: Liturgical Press, 1992), 2–3, points out, the canonical text of Acts is derived from the evidence supplied by many ancient manuscripts including fragmentary papyri from the third century. But while manuscripts display a considerable range of minor variations within a framework of substantial agreement, in the case of Acts, there is a smaller body of manuscripts called the Western Text Tradition (Codex D) that presents a rather consistent alternative version. In fact, Witherington, "The Anti-Feminist Tendencies of the 'Western' Text in Acts," 82, avers where Luke gives or appears to give noticeable attention to women (and particularly prominent women) "D" attempts to tone down or eliminate such reference.

16. During a visit to Philippi our guide emphasized the importance of the *ikon* to Byzantine Christianity. "You may forget the words," she said, "but you will never forget the face. It impels you." This is exactly what I hope Craighead's depiction of Priscilla and Aquila will do for us.

17. John S. Dunne, *A Search for God in Time and Memory* (London: The Macmillan Company, 1970), viii–ix.

18. See John H. Elliott, "Jesus The Israelite Was Neither A 'Jew' Nor A 'Christian': On Correcting Misleading Nomenclature," *Journal for the Study of the Historical Jesus* 5, no. 2 (2007): 119–54, for an elaboration on this assertion.

Chapter 1, pages 1–27

1. Richard Horsley, *1 Corinthians* (Nashville, TN: Abingdon Press, 1998), 28–29. Ernst Haenchen (*The Acts of the Apostles: A Commentary* [Philadelphia: Westminster Press, 1971], 538) agrees. Whereas, Jerome Murphy-O'Connor ("Prisca and Aquila: Travelling Tentmakers and Church Builders," *Bible Review* [December 1992]: 48) thinks Paul arrived in Corinth in the spring of 50, while Ben Witherington III (*The Acts of the Apostles: A Socio-Rhetorical Commentary* [Grand Rapids, MI: Eerdmans, 1998], 551) and F. F. Bruce (*The Book of the Acts*, New International Commentary on the New Testament, rev. ed.

[Grand Rapids, MI: Eerdmans, 1988], 351) assert he was there from the fall of 50 to the spring of 52. Finally, Joseph A. Fitzmyer (*The Acts of the Apostles*, Anchor Bible 31 [Garden City, NY: Doubleday, 1998], 623) posits Paul could have been hauled before Gallio as late as the fall of 52. Each scholar's date is based on their interpretation of the Gallio inscription(s). See Fitzmyer, *The Acts of the Apostles*, 620–23, for a detailed synopsis on the dating of Gallio's consulship. Then go to www.kchanson.com/ANCDOCS/greek/gallio.html for a translation of the text. The original text is in the Museum at Delphi.

2. Fitzmyer, *The Acts of the Apostles*, 241, describes the area: Pontus was originally the name of the Black Sea, but it came to designate the area bordering on that sea in the northeastern part of Asia Minor. The area was earlier an empire founded by Achaemenid Persians, reaching from the Black Sea to the Caucasus. After Pompey conquered it, part of it became the Roman province of Pontus. Many Greeks were known to have settled there and, with them, Greek-speaking Jews (cf. 1 Pet 1:1). Richard M. Soule, "Co-Workers: Prisca and Aquila," *Ekklesia: Then and Now* 62 (October 18, 2005), 1, thinks Aquila may have come from Sinope, which was a town that had a large Jewish population.

3. The fact that Aquila is in Rome suggests to W. M. Ramsey, *St Paul the Traveller and the Roman Citizen* (London: Hodder and Stoughton, 1895), 253f., that Aquila is a Roman from the Roman province of Pontus. Robert Jewett, *Romans: A Commentary*, Hermeneia (Minneapolis: Fortress, 2007), 957f., goes a step further and posits both he *and* Priscilla were Roman citizens, while Bruce J. Malina and John J. Pilch, *Social-Science Commentary on the Book of Acts* (Minneapolis: Fortress Press, 2008), 130, aver that the forcible emigration of Priscilla and Aquila confirms Aquila was not a Roman citizen.

4. Murphy-O'Connor, "Prisca and Aquila: Travelling Tentmakers and Church Builders," 42–44, posits Aquila was a freed slave of the same family Priscilla was, since the Latin name Acilius was sometimes written Aquilius, from which Aquila is easily derived. Prisca and its diminutive Priscilla were also common names/*cognomina* in the family and so as freed slaves they would have typically adopted these names from their master's family. While Bruce (*The Book of Acts*, 348n15) contends there was no reason to connect this Priscilla with the woman of the same name after which the Cemetery of Priscilla on the Via Salaria, one of the earliest Christian catacombs in Rome, is named. Nor should the name of Aquila be connected with the Acilii Glabriones, a noble Roman family that owned a crypt in the cemetery. See also Peter Lampe, "Prisca," *ABD* 5 (New York: Doubleday, 1992), 468.

5. See Peter Lampe, *From Paul to Valentinus: Christians at Rome in the First Two Centuries*, trans. Michael Steinhauser (Minneapolis: Fortress Press, 2003), 153–83, for an enunciation of his point. See also Peter Lampe, "Aquila," *ABD* 1 (New York: Doubleday, 1992), 319; and "Prisca," *ABD* 5, 467.

6. Ross Shepard Kraemer, *Her Share of the Blessings: Women's Religions among Pagans, Jews, and Christians in the Greco-Roman World* (New York: Oxford University Press, 1992), 136–38, is an example.

7. See Margaret Y. MacDonald, "Reading Real Women through the Undisputed Letters of Paul," in *Women and Christian Origins*, ed. Ross Shepard Kraemer and Mary Rose D'Angelo (New York: Oxford University Press, 1999), 202–3. See footnotes 5 and 6 on page 218 for a bibliography on this issue.

8. Mary Rose D'Angelo, "Women Partners in the New Testament," *Journal of Feminist Studies in Religion* 6, no. 1 (1990): 73–74, is an example.

9. Wayne A. Meeks, *The First Urban Christians: The Social World of the Apostle Paul* (New Haven, CT: Yale University Press, 1983), 57, 60. Carolyn Osiek and Margaret Y. MacDonald (*A Woman's Place: House Churches in Earliest Christianity* [Minneapolis: Fortress Press, 2006], 28) say, "It seems likely that Priscilla and Aquila (Rom 16:3; 1 Cor 16:19), Andronicus and Junia (Rom 16:7), and Philologus and Julia (Rom 16:15) understood themselves and were understood by others in the Pauline movement as married." See Kraemer, *Her Share of the Blessings*, 136–37, for an opposing view.

10. Cited from Richard Mott Gummere, trans., *Moral Letters to Lucilius by Seneca*, vol. 1 (Cambridge, MA: Harvard University Press, 1917), 27–29. See also www.stoics.com.

11. Paul lists his rights to food and drink provided by host churches along with his right to refrain from working for a living (1 Cor 9:4-6) as rights he does not use. Thus, the right to have a "wife" alongside him as a partner must mean that he has a right to have a wife travel with him at the expense of the churches.

12. Hans Conzelmann, *1 Corinthians*, Hermaneia, trans. James W. Leitch (Philadelphia: Fortress Press, 1975), 153n19. Conzelmann also mentions that at least one scholar thinks "sister" was added to the text at a later date.

13. Ibid., 119.

14. Gordon Fee, *The First Epistle to the Corinthians*, NICNT (Grand Rapids, MI: Eerdmans, 1987), 397; Horsley, *1 Corinthians*, 125; Marion Soards, *1 Corinthians*, New International Biblical Commentary (Peabody, MA: Hendrickson, 1999), 183–84.

15. MacDonald, "Reading Real Women," 203.

16. Oseik and MacDonald, *A Woman's Place*, 28.

17. See Witherington, *The Acts of the Apostles*, 539–44, for an exhaustive history of Roman relations with the Jews. See also, Harry J. Leon, *The Jews of Ancient Rome*, updated ed. (Peabody, MA: Hendrickson, 1994), 15–28; Wolfgang Weifel, "The Jewish Community in Ancient Rome and the Origins of Roman Christianity," in *The Romans Debate*, ed. Karl P. Donfried, rev. ed. (Peabody, MA: Hendrickson, 1991), 86–89; and Lampe, *From Paul to Valentinus*, 11–16.

18. Fitzmyer, *Acts of the Apostles*, 620.

19. Ernst Haenchen, *The Acts of the Apostles*, 538. Luke Timothy Johnson, *Acts of the Apostles*, Sacra Pagina 5 (Collegeville, MN: Liturgical Press, 1992), 322.

20. William J. Lane, "Social Perspective on Roman Christianity during the Formative Years from Nero to Nerva: Romans, Hebrews, 1 Clement," in *Judaism and Christianity in First-Century Rome*, eds. Karl P. Donfried and Peter Richardson (Grand Rapids, MI: Eerdmans, 1998), 205.

21. Harry J. Leon, *The Jews of Ancient Rome*, 135, especially note 1. Cf. Raymond E. Brown and John P. Meier, *Antioch and Rome: New Testament Cradles of Catholic Christianity* (New York: Paulist Press, 1982), 94.

22. Leon, *The Jews of Ancient Rome*, 257.

23. Ibid., 93–121.

24. Bruce, *The Book of the Acts of the Apostles*, 347.

25. F. F. Bruce, "The Romans Debate—Continued," in *The Romans Debate*, ed. Karl P. Donfried, rev. and exp. ed. (Peabody, MA: Hendrickson, 1991), 179.

26. Lampe, *From Paul to Valentinus*, 12. See also, F. F. Bruce, "The Romans Debate—Continued," 177–86.

27. Wiefel,"The Jewish Community in Ancient Rome," 92. See also Lampe, "The 'Edit of Claudius' and the Separation from the Synagogue," in *From Paul to Valentinus*, 11–16.

28. Elisabeth Schüssler Fiorenza, "Missionaries, Apostles, Co-Workers: Romans 16 and the Reconstruction of Women's Early Church History," *Word and World* 6, no. 4 (1986): 429.

29. Haenchen, *The Acts of the Apostles*, 533.

30. Murphy-O'Connor, "Prisca and Aquila: Travelling Tentmakers," 49.

31. Witherington, *The Acts of the Apostles*, 565.

32. Indeed, Johnson, *Acts of the Apostles*, 322, suggests that Claudius' edict, which he believes was issued in 49 CE, is one of the key dates for establishing the possibility of an absolute chronology for Paul's career.

33. As Brian M. Rapske, "Acts, Travel and Shipwreck," in *The Book of Acts in Its First Century Setting*, vol. 2, *The Book of Acts in Its Graeco-Roman Setting*, ed. David W. J. Gill and Conrad Gempf (Grand Rapids, MI: Eerdmans, 1994), 22, indicates: The period from May 27 to September 14 was the safest season to travel. Periods from March 10 to May 26 and from September 14 to November 11 were when weather and sea conditions were quite changeable and so considered risky, and the period from November 11 to March 10 was extremely dangerous.

34. Jerome Murphy-O'Connor, *Paul: A Critical Life* (Oxford: Clarendon Press, 1966), 259.

35. See W. Michaelis, "*skēne*," TDNT, 7, 368–94, for a detailed analysis.

36. Ivoni Richter Reimer, "The Missionary Artisan Priscilla and the Universal Praise that Is Her Due (18:1-3,18-19, 24-28)," in *Women in Acts of the*

Apostles: A Feminist Liberation Perspective, trans. Linda M. Maloney (Minneapolis: Fortress Press, 1995), 200–201, for a review of the scholarship. Cf. Lampe, *From Paul to Valentinus*, 188–89.

37. Reimer, "The Missionary Artisan," 202–3.

38. Rapske, "Acts, Travel and Shipwreck," 7.

39. Ronald F. Hock, *The Social Context of Paul's Ministry: Tentmaking and Apostleship* (Philadelphia: Fortress Press, 1980), 21. Cf. Michaelis, "*skēne*," TDNT 7, 394; Marshall, *Acts*, 293; and Haenchen, *The Acts of the Apostles*, 534.

40. Murphy-O'Connor, "Prisca and Aquila: Traveling Tentmakers," 44f.

41. David E. Malick, "The Contribution of Codex Bezae Cantabrigiensis to an Understanding of Women in The Book of Acts," *Journal of Greco-Roman Christianity and Judaism* 4 (2007): 179f.: "In v.2 Codex B reads: 'He approached them' but Codex D reads, 'Paul approached him [Aquila]'. Although subtle, this change seems to focus upon Paul approaching the man and not the woman. This variant reflects the bias in Codex D to move women, in this case Priscilla, out of the center of the activity." D also adds that Aquila was of the same tribe as Paul. Moreover, "In v.3, Codex B reads, 'they were working' using the third person plural imperfect of *ergazomai*, while Codex D says that only Paul worked, using the third person singular of *ergazomai*. Codex D also deletes the phrase from Codex B 'for they were tent-makers by trade'. These small changes all have the effect of removing Priscilla out of the reader's view. In this initial introduction, Priscilla is only identified as Aquila's wife. Then in Codex D, Paul is not approaching 'them' as a couple, but only the man, Aquila. In addition, they (meaning Paul, Aquila and Priscilla) are not working their craft together, only Paul is working. And that is because they (Paul, Aquila and Priscilla) do not even share a craft together as tentmakers. Instead of making Paul a partner with the husband-and-wife team of Aquila and Priscilla, Paul is described as working with a man, Aquila, who happens to also have a wife named Priscilla."

42. Michaelis (TDNT 7, 394) thinks it is more probable that Paul and Aquila were leatherworkers and that they manufactured tents, for which there was considerable use in antiquity.

43. Hock, "Social Context of Paul's Ministry," chap. 3, 81n46, contends that it is difficult to determine whether Priscilla was also understood by Luke's tradition to have been a tentmaker alongside her husband, but I think not. Had tents been a product of weavers, the likelihood would be better, since weaving was often, though not exclusively, a woman's trade (so Xenophon *Oec.* 7.5, 41; 10.10; Musonius *frag.* [p 46, 13-27, Lutz]; Juvenal *Sat.* 11.69; Lucian *D. Meretr.*6.293; and Diogenes Laertius 6.98). Obviously, Hock thinks tentmaking was too hard for women.

44. Notice chap. 18 titled "Aquila and Prisca" in *From Paul to Valentinus* (187–95) is mostly about Aquila.

45. Murphy-O'Connor, "Prisca and Aquila: Travelling Tentmakers," 48. He also includes a fine illustration.

46. Hock, "The Social Context of Paul's Ministry," 32. An example of this can be seen in Peter Connolly, *Pompeii* (Oxford: Oxford University Press, 1990), 54f. Here he illustrates the reconstruction of the shop of the bronze-smith Verus. Like many others, it had living quarters above that were reached by wooden stairs from a masonry foundation.

47. Catherine Clark Kroeger, trans. "John Chrysostom's First Homily on the Greeting to Priscilla and Aquila," *Priscilla Papers* 5, no. 3 (1991): 17.

48. Luise Schottroff, "Women as Followers of Jesus in New Testament Times," in *The Bible and Liberation: Political and Social Hermeneutics*, ed. Norman K. Gottwald and Richard Horsley (Maryknoll, NY: Orbis, 1993), 458–59.

49. See Reimer, "The Missionary Artisan Priscilla," 205–6, for an analysis of their positions.

50. Meeks, *The First Urban Christians*, 59, claims that their wealth was "relatively high," even though their occupation was "low, but not at the bottom." He bases his assertion on the fact that they were able to move from place to place, establish a sizable household in three different cities, and act as patrons for Paul and the Christian congregation.

51. Reimer, "The Missionary Artisan Priscilla," 206. Cf. Lampe, *From Paul to Valentinus*, 19. I would concur.

52. Reimer, "The Missionary Artisan Priscilla," 207.

53. Lampe, *From Paul to Valentinus*, 189.

54. Ibid., 192. Moreover, Murphy-O'Connor, "Prisca and Aquila: Travelling Tentmakers," 49, asserts they are similar to the shops found in Ostia and elsewhere so that a generic description of them is valid for all major towns throughout the empire.

55. Murphy-O'Connor, *Paul: A Critical Life*, 263.

56. Haenchen, *The Acts of the Apostles*, 538–39. Moreover, Haenchen's observation is in accord with Priscilla and Aquila's later activity as recorded by Paul in Ephesus (1 Cor 16:19 from Ephesus) and Rome (Rom 16:3-5). As far as Luke's narrative is concerned, however, all light must fall on Paul.

57. Murphy-O'Connor, "Prisca and Aquila: Travelling Tentmakers," 50.

58. Lampe, *From Paul to Valentinus*, 193.

59. Bruce, *The Book of Acts*, 354.

60. Murphy-O'Connor, "Prisca and Aquila: Travelling Tentmakers," 50–51.

61. See Paul Trebilco, "Asia," in *The Book of Acts in Its First-Century Setting*, vol. 2, *Graeco-Roman Setting*, ed. David W. J. Gill and Conrad Gempf (Grand Rapids, MI: Eerdmans, 1994), 291–362, for a comprehensive look at the history and importance of Ephesus.

62. F. Scott Spencer, "Women of 'the Cloth' in Acts: Sewing the Word," in *The Feminist Companion to the Acts of the Apostles*, ed. Amy-Jill Levine and Marianne Blickenstaff (Cleveland, OH: Pilgrim Press, 2004), 152.

63. Witherington, *The Acts of the Apostles*, 566.

64. Kroeger, "John Chrysostom's First Homily," 18. Chrysostom raises Priscilla up not only here but again in Homily 10 on Second Timothy and in Homily 40 on Acts of the Apostles (18:18). Considering he was known for making many statements against women, this is remarkable!

65. According to Bruce, *The Book of Acts*, 360: The Western Text (D) adds that Apollos was invited by some Corinthians who had made his acquaintance in Ephesus to move to Corinth. Moreover, "D" discounts that Priscilla and Aquila had anything to do with writing his recommendation. Instead "D" posits that Ephesians (i.e., Paul's first converts) wrote to the disciples asking them to welcome him.

66. Malina and Pilch, *Social Science Commentary on the Book of Acts*, 135, enunciate the importance of a letter of recommendation: "For such a letter assured fellow believers in other regions that the traveler the letter recommended (who was a stranger to them) was deserving of hospitality and did not have to be 'tested' according to the cultural rules for extending hospitality." See Rom 16:1 and 2 Cor 3:1 for examples of the importance of a letter of recommendation.

Chapter 2, pages 28–56

1. I am indebted to Richard M. Soule, *Ekklessia, Then and Now*, #23, January 6, 2004, for the map included here, and I acknowledge his gracious permission to use it.

2. While canonically this letter is called Paul's "First Letter to the Corinthians," we know from the text that Paul is answering questions the Corinthian community asked him that arose from a previous letter that has been lost to us. Paul's answers begin in chapter 7.

3. Gordon D. Fee, *The First Epistle to the Corinthians*, The New International Commentary on the New Testament (Grand Rapids, MI: Eerdmans, 1987), 835.

4. Jesus believers were not the only religious group that met in houses; in the first part of the twentieth century, archaeologists discovered three homes in Dura Europos, Syria, that were renovated for use as religious buildings. One became a mithraeum, another a synagogue, and the last a third-century church. It is the earliest complete extant church.

5. Floyd Filson, "The Significance of Early House Churches," *Journal of Biblical Literature* 58 (1939): 105–12.

6. Houses have always been used as places to support and sustain belief. During the Communist regime in Poland, for example, Catholics met in secret in one another's houses to pray with, support, and encourage one another. Karol Józef Wojtyła, later Pope John Paul II, met with others in one of them.

7. Vincent Branick, *The House Church in the Writings of Paul*, Zacchaeus Studies: New Testament, ed. Mary Ann Getty (Wilmington, DE: Michael Glazier, 1989), 15, proffers that by the mid–second century early believers had moved from using space in their homes to dedicating their homes, which they no longer lived in, to the needs of the church assembly. This practice continued until they were allowed to build churches from the ground up. An example of a third-century church at Dura-Europos can be viewed at http://deeperstudy.com/link/dura_church.html.

8. See Santiago Guijarro, "The Family in First-Century Galilee," in *Constructing Early Christian Families: Family as Social Reality and Metaphor*, ed. Halvor Moxnes (New York: Routledge, 1997), 49–55, for information and diagrams of the type of houses that existed in Palestine during the Roman-Byzantine periods.

9. Roger W. Gehring, *House Church and Mission: The Importance of Household Structures in Early Christianity* (Peabody, MA: Hendrickson, 2004), 65.

10. Indeed, the descriptions of the fourteen administrative regions into which Emperor Augustus divided Rome listed only one private house for every twenty-six blocks of *insulae*.

11. James S. Jeffers, "Jewish and Christian Families in First-Century Rome," in *Judaism and Christianity in First-Century Rome*, ed. Karl P. Donfried and Peter Richardson (Grand Rapids, MI: Eerdmans, 1998), 132.

12. David Verner, *The Household of God: The Social World of the Pastoral Epistles*, SBL Dissertation Series 71, ed. William Baird (Chico, CA: Scholars Press, 1983), 57.

13. Freed slaves normally continued to serve their masters. Some continued to live with them, while others ended up in the upper floors of an *insulae*.

14. See Jerome Murphy-O'Connor, *St. Paul's Corinth: Text And Archaeology*. 3rd rev. and exp. ed. (Collegeville, MN: Liturgical Press, 2002), 178–85, for a good analysis of the space involved.

15. Branick, *The House Church in the Writings of Paul*, 15.

16. See chapter 2, "Households in the Hellenistic-Roman World," 27–82, in Verner, *The Household of God*, for a detailed description.

17. J. Albert Harrill, *Slaves in the New Testament: Literary, Social, and Moral Dimensions* (Minneapolis: Fortress Press, 2006), 97–103, claims these codes

were also available in agricultural handbooks, such as Xenephon, *Oeconomicus*; Varro, *De re rustica*; and Colomella, *De re rustica.*

18. See *Laudatio Turiae* LS 8393, col.i, 11.30-3. Cited in Geoffrey S. Nathan, *The Family in Late Antiquity: The Rise of Christianity and the Endurance of Tradition* (London: Routledge, 2000), 196.

19. See Sarah B. Pomeroy, *Plutarch's Advice to the Bride and Groom, and a Consolation to His Wife* (Oxford: Oxford University Press, 1999), for an English translation, commentary, and bibliography on this important essay.

20. Using Paul's letter to Philemon, Karl Olav Sandes shows how Paul expects that the eschatological brother-sisterhood of equality should have an effect on the social system of the household. Cf. "Equality Within Patriarchal Structures: Some New Testament Perspectives on the Christian Fellowship as a Brother- or Sisterhood and a Family," in Moxnes, *Constructing Early Christian Families*, 150–65.

21. It is interesting to note, as Ben Witherington III does (*Women in the Earliest Churches* [New York: Cambridge University Press, 1988], 106), that it was not at all common in Judaism to call one's fellow believers brothers or sisters, nor was this the practice in other groups such as the Dionysians. But this practice was fundamental to the early Jesus believers, and there was a real feeling among them that they were a family of faith.

22. Elisabeth Schüssler Fiorenza, *In Memory of Her: A Feminist Theological Reconstruction of Christian Origins* (New York: Crossroads, 1987), chaps. 5 and 6; and David Balch, *Let Wives Be Submissive: The Domestic Code in 1 Peter* (Atlanta, GA: Scholars Press, 1981), 28–36, are two examples.

23. A form of the household codes also appears in 1 Peter 2:18-3:7. Written in the last part of the first century, this letter is addressed to Jesus believers in Asia Minor at a time when foreign cults were suspect. Its author gives basic advice to those who want to maintain their integrity as Christ followers at the same time that they are living openly and actively in the world. Wives and slaves living in the households of unbelievers are especially addressed. John H. Elliott, *A Home for the Homeless: A Sociological Exegesis of 1 Peter, Its Situation and Strategy* (Philadelphia: Fortress, 1981), details the way in which the household codes fit into the writer's strategy.

24. See Virginia Ramey-Mollenkott, "Emancipative Elements in Ephesians 5:21-33: Why Feminist Scholarship Has (Often) Left Them Unmentioned, and Why They Should Be Emphasized," in *A Feminist Companion to the Deutero-Pauline Epistles*, ed. Amy-Jill Levine and Marianne Blickenstaff (Cleveland, OH: The Pilgrim Press, 2003), 36–58, for a thoughtful elaboration.

25. In their case, the authors of the letters in which the "codes" appear seem to be looking to change the attitudes and perspectives of the "players" in the house, for it was quite another thing to change the social system of

the household. For as Dennis C. Duling ("'Egalitarian' Ideology, Leadership, and Factional Conflict Within the Matthean Group," *Biblical Theology Bulletin* 27, no. 4 [1997]: 126), points out, ancient society was not "egalitarian" in the modern Enlightenment, individualist, political-philosophical sense in which equality is a self-evident human right and/or social goal for everyone. Cf. John H. Elliott, "Jesus Was Not an Egalitarian: A Critique of an Anachronistic and Idealist Theory," *BTB* 32, no. 2 (2002): 75–91.

26. Filson, "The Significance of Early House Churches," 106.

27. Note that Luke also uses the same phrase, "with one accord," to describe the attitude of the persecutors. Cf. Acts 7:52; 12:20; 18:12; 19:29.

28. Branick, *The House Church in the Writings of Paul*, 24.

29. I agree with those scholars who see Romans 16 as an integral part of Paul's letter. Ben Witherington III with Darlene Hyatt, *Paul's Letter to the Romans: A Socio-Rhetorical Commentary* (Grand Rapids, MI: Eerdmans, 2004), 5–6, is an example.

30. Peter Lampe, "The Roman Christians of Romans 16," in *The Romans Debate*, ed. Karl P. Donfried, rev. and exp. ed. (Peabody, MA: Hendrickson, 2006), 226. Such a situation also helps to explain the problems that arose in the community, since for the five or so years the Judean Christ believers were away, the Hellenist Jesus group grew and prospered, and as Romans attests, they didn't take kindly to their return. Cf. Rom 11:13-24.

31. Witherington, *Paul's Letter to the Romans*, 11. See Lampe, "The Roman Christians in Romans 16," 216–30, for an in-depth analysis of the makeup of this group.

32. Indeed, a lack of central coordination matches the profile of the separated synagogues in Rome.

33. William L. Lane, "Social Perspectives on Roman Christianity during the Formative Years from Nero to Nerva: Romans, Hebrews, 1 Clement," in *Judaism and Christianity in First-Century Rome*, ed. Karl P. Donfried and Peter Richardson (Grand Rapids, MI; Eerdmans, 1998), 213. Furthermore: "Ignatius and Hermas provide evidence that even in the first decades of the second century Rome was not centrally organized under the administrative authority of a single bishop. In six of his seven letters, Ignatius insists on the importance of the office of bishop. His silence in regard to this pastoral concern in the *Letter to the Romans* (ca. 110 C.E.) is explained best by the absence of a monarchical bishop in Rome. Hermas refers only to 'the elders who preside over the church' (*Herm. Vis* 2.43: 3.9.7). The existence of several house churches only loosely connected with one another throughout Rome suggests why diversity, disunity, and a tendency toward independence were persistent problems in the early church of the Christian Communities in Rome."

34. Gehring, *House Church and Mission*, 80.

35. Some scholars refer to this reference as a "fellowship meal," since the "breaking of bread" could refer to an ordinary Judean meal. However, as Witherington (*The Acts of the Apostles*, 160f.) points out:

> Theophilus will already have heard about the Last Supper meal in the first volume, and perhaps more importantly about the recognition of Jesus at the breaking of the bread in the (for Luke) crucial Emmaus road resurrection appearance story (Luke 24:35), which suggests Luke emphasizes the connection between Jesus' presence and such meals (cf. Luke 24:41-42; Acts 1:4; 10:41). Furthermore, texts like Acts 2:42, 46, and 20:7, 11 all suggest that this sort of breaking of bread was part of an act of worship that involved eating, praying, teaching, and singing in homes, to mention but a few elements of the service. On the whole, then, the phrase "the breaking of bread" seems to be a primitive way of alluding to the Lord's Supper, though it cannot be ruled out that the reference is to an ordinary meal.

36. Bonnie Thurston, *Spiritual Life in the Early Church: The Witness of Acts and Ephesians* (Minneapolis: Augsburg Fortress, 1993), 23.

37. Branick, *The House Church in the Writings of Paul*, 94–95.

38. Brendan Byrne, *Romans*, ed. Daniel J. Harrington, Sacra Pagina (Collegeville, MN: Liturgical Press, 2007), 29, 446–47.

39. Keith A. Gerberding, "Women Who Toil in Ministry, Even as Paul," *Currents in Theology and Mission* 18, no. 4 (1991): 285. John Chrysostom captures this same notion in Homily 30 on Romans when he says Paul called Prisc(ill)a and Aquila his *sunergoi* "to point out that they had been sharers of his very great labors and dangers." Cf. J. Walker, J. Sheppard, and H. Browne, trans., and revised by George B. Stevens, *From Nicene and Post-Nicene Fathers*, vol. 11, First Series, ed. Philip Schaff (Buffalo, NY: Christian Literature Publishing Co., 1889). Revised and edited for New Advent by Kevin Knight, http://www.newadvent.org/fathers/210230.htm.

40. Ivoni Richter Reimer, "The Missionary Artisan Priscilla and the Universal Praise that Is Her Due (18:1-3.18-19, 24-28)," in *Women in Acts of the Apostles: A Feminist Liberation Perspective*, trans. Linda M. Maloney (Minneapolis: Fortress Press, 1995), 215.

41. See Bruce Malina, *Timothy: Paul's Closest Associate*, Paul's Social Network: Brothers and Sisters in Faith (Collegeville, MN: Liturgical Press, 2008), xi–xii, for the use of the word "Gentile."

42. Robert Jewett, *Romans: A Commentary*. Hermeneia. (Minneapolis: Fortress, 2007), 958.

43. Ibid.

44. See Luke Timothy Johnson, *Letter to Paul's Delegates: 1 Timothy, 2 Timothy, Titus*. The New Testament in Context, ed. Howard Clark Kee and

J. Andrew Overman (Valley Forge, PA: Trinity Press International, 1996), 1–36, for an overview of scholarly opinion; although in this instance Johnson hesitantly thinks Paul wrote all three letters. On the other hand, Jerome Murphy-O'Connor, *Paul: A Critical Life* (Oxford: Clarendon Press, 1996), 357, argues for the authenticity of 2 Timothy but claims followers of Paul wrote the other two letters using 2 Timothy as a model.

45. Mentioning Pris(cill)a's name is especially onerous for this writer, even as he establishes authenticity and credibility for his work by mentioning her. For as Bonnie Thurston (*Women in the New Testament: Questions and Commentary* [New York: Crossroads, 1998], 144) points out, by doing so, he reminds his readers of a woman who does not really follow the injunctions given to women in 1 Tim 2:11-15, where they are forbidden to teach. Apparently his desire for establishing historical credibility outweighed his need for strict consistency.

46. Philip Schaff, ed. and trans., *From Nicene and Post-Nicene Fathers*, vol. 13, First Series (Buffalo, NY: Christian Literature Publishing, Co., 1889). Revised and edited for New Advent by Kevin Knight, http://www.newadvent.org/fathers/230710.htm.

Chapter 3, pages 57–63

1. See Bruce J. Malina, *The New Testament World: Insights from Cultural Anthropology*, rev. ed. (Louisville, KY: Westminster John Knox, 1993), 28–62, for an excursus on the importance of this pivotal value.

2. I have adapted the work of Frederick Danker, *Luke*, Proclamation Commentaries, ed. Gerhard Krodel, 2nd rev. and enlarged ed. (Philadelphia: Fortress Press, 1987), 28–46, on "Exceptional Merit and Beneficence." Danker uses the material to show how Luke presents Jesus. I think it can apply to Priscilla and Aquila as well.

3. Ibid., 29–30. Both the letter and decree have been translated by Danker. Cf. Frederick W. Danker, "Letter of Paulus Fabius Maximus and Decrees by Asians Concerning the Provincial Calendar," in *Benefactor: Epigraphic Study of a Graeco-Roman and New Testament Semantic Field* (St. Louis, MO: Clayton Publishing House, 1982), 215–22.

4. Ibid., 31.

5. Catherine Clark Kroeger, trans., "John Chrysostom's First Homily on the Greeting to Priscilla and Aquila," *Priscilla Papers* 5, no. 3 (1991): 17.

6. Danker, *Luke*, 38. Cf. "The Decree by the People of Dionysopolis in Honor of Akornion, Priest and Envoy," in Danker, *Benefactor*, 77–79.

7. Danker, *Luke*, 38. Cf. "Decree by Sestos in Honor of Menas, Son of Menes, Envoy, Gymnasiarch, and Supervisor of the Coinage," in Danker, *Benefactor*, 92–97.

Chapter 4, pages 64–74

1. Ivoni Richter Reimer, "The Missionary Artisan Priscilla and the Universal Praise that Is Her Due (18:1-3,18-19, 24-28)," in *Women in Acts of the Apostles: A Feminist Liberation Perspective*, trans. Linda M. Maloney (Minneapolis: Fortress Press, 1995), 216.

2. David DeLambo, *Lay Parish Ministers: A Study of Emerging Leadership* (New York: National Parish Life Center, 2006), 145.

3. Carolyn Osiek and Margaret Y. MacDonald, *A Woman's Place: House Churches in Earliest Christianity* (Minneapolis: Fortress Press, 2006), 32.

4. Robert P. Maloney, "Priscilla and Aquila Set Out Again: A Profile of the Lay Catholic in the 21st Century," *America Magazine*, 188, no. 8 (March 10, 2003): 8.

5. James and Evelyn Whitehead, *Method in Ministry: Theological Reflection and Christian Ministry*, rev. ed. (Franklin, WI: Sheed and Ward, 1999), 95.

6. Ibid.

7. Maloney, "Priscilla and Aquila Set Out Again," 9.

8. Ibid.

9. Brendan Byrne, *Romans*, ed. Daniel J. Harrington, Sacra Pagina (Collegeville, MN: Liturgical Press, 2007), 12, posits that Paul wrote to the Roman community to remind them, on the basis of the gospel, of the true relationship between Judean believers and non-Judean believers within the one people of God.

10. Please see Dominika A. Kurek-Chomycz, "Is There an 'Anti-Priscan' Tendency in the Manuscripts? Some Textual Problems with Prisca and Aquila," *Journal of Biblical Literature* 1 (2006): 107–28, for a full review.

11. Reimer, "The Missionary Artisan Priscilla," 216.

12. Ibid., 217.

Conclusion, pages 75–76

1. Cited from Richard Mott Gummere, trans., *Moral Letters to Lucilius by Seneca*, vol. 1 (Cambridge, MA: Harvard University Press, 1917), 63–65. See also www.stoics.com.

BIBLIOGRAPHY

Balch, David L. *Let Wives Be Submissive: The Domestic Code of 1 Peter.* Atlanta, GA: Scholars Press, 1981.

Banks, Robert. *Paul's Idea of Community: The Early House Churches in Their Historical Setting.* Grand Rapids, MI: Eerdmans, 1980.

Belleville, Linda L. "Women Leaders in the Bible." In *Discovering Biblical Equality: Complementarity without Hierarchy.* Edited by Ronald W. Pierce and Rebecca Merrill Groothuis, 110–25. Downers Grove, IL: IVP Academic, 2005.

Benedict XVI, General Audience, February 7, 2007.

Branick, Vincent. *The House Church in the Writings of Paul.* Wilmington, DE: Michael Glazier, 1989.

Brown, Raymond E., and John P. Meier. *Antioch and Rome: New Testament Cradles of Catholic Christianity.* New York: Paulist Press, 1982.

Bruce, F. F. *The Book of the Acts.* New International Commentary on the New Testament. Rev. ed. Grand Rapids, MI: Eerdmans, 1988.

———. "The Romans Debate—Continued." In *The Romans Debate*, edited by Karl P. Donfried, 175–94. Rev. and exp. ed. Peabody, MA: Hendrickson, 1991.

Byrne, Brendan. *Romans.* Sacra Pagina 6. Collegeville, MN: Liturgical Press, 2007.

Chambers, Talbot W., trans. John Chrysostom's Homily 44 on First Corinthians (16:10–16:24). *From Nicene and Post-Nicene Fathers.* Vol. 12. First Series. Edited by Philip Schaff. Buffalo, NY: Christian Literature Publishing Co, 1889. Revised and edited for New Advent by Kevin Knight. http://www.newadvent.org/fathers/220144.htm.

Connolly, Peter. *Pompeii.* Oxford: Oxford University Press, 1990.

Conzelmann, Hans. *1 Corinthians*. Hermaneia. Translated by James W. Leitch. Philadelphia: Fortress Press, 1975.

D'Angelo, Mary Rose. "Women Partners in the New Testament." *Journal of Feminist Studies in Religion* 6, no. 1 (1990): 65–86.

Danker, Frederick W. *Benefactor: Epigraphic Study of a Graeco-Roman and New Testament Semantic Field*. St. Louis, MO: Clayton Publishing House, 1982.

———. *Luke*. Edited by Gerhard Krodel. Proclamation Commentaries. 2nd rev. and exp. ed. Philadelphia: Fortress Press, 1987.

DeLambo, David. *Lay Parish Ministers: A Study of Emerging Leadership*. New York: National Parish Life Center, 2006.

Duling, Dennis C. "'Egalitarian' Ideology, Leadership, and Factional Conflict within the Matthean Group." *Biblical Theology Bulletin* 27, no. 4 (1997): 124–39.

Dunne, John S. *A Search for God in Time and Memory*. London: The Macmillan Company, 1970.

Elliott, John H. *A Home for the Homeless: A Sociological Exegesis of 1 Peter Its Situation and Strategy*. Philadelphia: Fortress, 1981.

———. "Jesus The Israelite Was Neither A 'Jew' Nor A 'Christian': On Correcting Misleading Nomenclature." *Journal for the Study of the Historical Jesus* vol. 5 (2007): 119–54.

———. "Jesus Was Not an Egalitarian: A Critique of an Anachronistic and Idealist Theory." *Biblical Theology Bulletin* 32, no. 2 (2002): 75–91.

Fee, Gordon. *The First Epistle to the Corinthians*. NICNT. Grand Rapids, MI: Eerdmans, 1987.

Filson, Floyd. "The Significance of Early House Churches." *Journal of Biblical Literature* 58 (1939): 105–12.

Fiorenza, Elisabeth Schüssler. *In Memory of Her: A Feminist Theological Reconstruction of Christian Origins.* New York: Crossroads, 1987.

———. "Missionaries, Apostles, Coworkers: Romans 16 and the Reconstruction of Women's Early Christian History." *Word and World* 6, no. 4 (1986): 420–33.

Fitzmyer, Joseph A. *The Acts of the Apostles*. Anchor Bible 31. Garden City, NY: Doubleday, 1998.

Gaventa, Beverly Roberts. *Acts.* Nashville, TN: Abingdon Press, 2003.

Gehring, Roger W. *House Church and Mission: The Importance of Household Structures in Early Christianity.* Peabody, MA: Hendrickson, 2004.

Gerberding, Keith A. "Women Who Toil in Ministry, Even as Paul" *Currents in Theology and Mission* 18, no. 4 (1991): 285–91.

Getty-Sullivan, Mary Ann. *Women in the New Testament.* Collegeville, MN: Liturgical Press, 2001.

Guijarro, Santiago. "The Family in First-Century Galilee." In *Constructing Early Christian Families: Family as Social Reality and Metaphor*, edited by Halvor Moxnes, 42–65. New York: Routledge, 1997.

Gummere, Richard Mott, trans. *Moral Letters to Lucilius by Seneca.* Vol. 1. Cambridge, MA: Harvard University Press, 1917. www.stoics .com.

Haenchen, Ernst. *The Acts of the Apostles: A Commentary.* Philadelphia: Westminster Press, 1971.

Harrill, J. Albert. *Slaves in the New Testament: Literary, Social, and Moral Dimensions.* Minneapolis: Fortress Press, 2006.

Hock, Ronald F. *The Social Context of Paul's Ministry: Tentmaking and Apostleship.* Philadelphia: Fortress Press, 1980.

Horsley, Richard. *1 Corinthians.* Nashville, TN: Abingdon Press, 1998.

Jeffers, James S. "Jewish and Christian Families in First-Century Rome." In *Judaism and Christianity in First-Century Rome*, edited by Karl P. Donfried and Peter Richardson, 128–50. Grand Rapids, MI: Eerdmans, 1998.

Jewett, Robert. *Romans: A Commentary.* Hermeneia. Minneapolis: Fortress Press, 2007.

Johnson, Luke Timothy. *Acts of the Apostles.* Sacra Pagina 5. Collegeville, MN: Liturgical Press, 1992.

———. *Letters to Paul's Delegates: 1 Timothy, 2 Timothy, Titus.* Edited by Howard Clark Kee and J. Andrew Overman. The New Testament in Context. Valley Forge, PA: Trinity Press International, 1996.

Kraemer, Ross Shepard. *Her Share of the Blessings*: *Women's Religions Among Pagans, Jews, and Christians in the Graeo-Roman World.* New York: Oxford University Press, 1992.

Kroeger, Catherine Clark, trans. "John Chrysostom's First Homily on the Greeting to Priscilla and Aquila." *Priscilla Papers* 5, no. 3 (1991): 16–20.

Kurek-Chomycz, Dominika. "Is There an 'Anti-Priscan' Tendency in the Manuscripts? Some Textual Problems with Priscilla and Aquila." *Journal of Biblical Literature* 125 (2006): 107–28.

Lampe, Peter. "Aquila." In *Anchor Bible Dictionary*, 1:319–20. New York: Doubleday, 1992.

————. *From Paul to Valentinus: Christians at Rome in the First Two Centuries*, translated by Michael Steinhauser. Minneapolis: Fortress, 2003.

————. "Prisca." In *Anchor Bible Dictionary*, 5:467–68. New York: Doubleday, 1992.

————. "The Roman Christians of Romans 16." In *The Romans Debate*, edited by Karl P. Donfried, 216–30. Rev. and exp. ed. Peabody, MA: Hendrickson, 1991.

Lane, William J. "Social Perspective on Roman Christianity during the Formative Years from Nero to Nerva: Romans, Hebrews, 1 Clement." In *Judaism and Christianity in First-Century Rome*, edited by Karl P. Donfried and Peter Richardson, 196–244. Grand Rapids, MI: Eerdmans, 1998.

Leon, Harry J. *The Jews of Ancient Rome.* Updated ed. Peabody, MA: Hendrickson, 1995.

MacDonald, Margaret Y. "Reading Real Women through the Undisputed Letters of Paul." In *Women and Christian Origins*, edited by Ross Shepard Kraemer and Mary Rose D'Angelo, 199–220. New York: Oxford University Press, 1999.

Malick, David E. "The Contribution of Codex Bezae Cantabrigiensis to an Understanding of Women in the Book of Acts." In *Journal of Greco-Roman Christianity and Judaism* 4 (2007): 158–83.

Malina, Bruce J. *The New Testament World: Insights from Cultural Anthropology.* 3rd ed. Louisville, KY: Westminster John Knox Press, 2001.

————. *Timothy: Paul's Closest Associate.* Paul's Social Network: Brothers and Sisters in Faith. Collegeville, MN: Liturgical Press, 2008.

————, and John J. Pilch. *Social-Science Commentary on the Book of Acts.* Minneapolis: Fortress Press, 2008.

Maloney, Robert P. "Priscilla and Aquila Set Out Again: A Profile of the Lay Catholic in the 21st Century." *America Magazine* 188, no. 8 (March 10, 2003): 7–9.

Marshal, I. Howard. *Acts.* Vol. 5. TNTC. Downers Grove, IL: IVP Academic, 1980.

Meeks, Wayne A. *The First Urban Christians: The Social World of the Apostle Paul.* New Haven, CT: Yale University Press, 1983.

Michaelis, W. "*skēne*, et al." TDNT 7, 368–94.

Murphy-O'Connor, Jerome. *Paul: A Critical Life.* Oxford: Clarendon Press, 1966.

————. "Prisca and Aquila: Traveling Tentmakers and Church Builders." *Bible Review* (December 1992): 40–51, 62.

————. *St. Paul's Corinth: Texts and Archaeology*. 3rd rev. and exp. ed.
Collegeville, MN: Liturgical Press, 2002.

Nathan, Geoffrey S. *The Family in Late Antiquity: The Rise of Christianity
and the Endurance of Tradition*. London: Routledge, 2000.

O'Day, Gail R. "Acts." In *Women's Bible Commentary*, edited by Carol A.
Newsom and Sharon H. Ringe, 394–402. Exp. ed. Louisville, KY:
Westminster John Knox Press, 1998.

Osiek, Carolyn, and Margaret Y. MacDonald. *A Woman's Place: House
Churches in Earliest Christianity*. Minneapolis: Fortress Press, 2006.

Pomeroy, Sarah. *Plutarch's Advice to the Bride and Groom and a Consolation
to His Wife*. Oxford: Oxford University Press, 1999.

Ramey-Mollenkott, Virginia. "Emancipative Elements in Ephesians
5:21-33: Why Feminist Scholarship Has (Often) Left Them Un-
mentioned, and Why They Should Be Emphasized." In *A Feminist
Companion to the Deutero-Pauline Epistles*, edited by Amy-Jill
Levine and Marianne Blickenstaff, 36–58. Cleveland, OH: The
Pilgrim Press, 2003.

Ramsey, W. M. *St Paul the Traveller and the Roman Citizen*. London: Hodder and Stoughton, 1895.

Rapske, Brian M. "Acts, Travel and Shipwreck." In *The Book of Acts in
Its First-Century Setting*, Vol. 2, *The Book of Acts in Its Graeco-Roman
Setting*, edited by David W. J. Gill and Conrad Gempf, 1–48.
Grand Rapids, MI: Eerdmans, 1994.

Reimer, Ivoni Richter. "The Missionary Artisan Priscilla and the Universal Praise that Is Her Due." In *Women in the Acts of the Apostles:
A Feminist Liberation Perspective*, translated by Linda M. Maloney,
195–226. Minneapolis: Fortress Press, 1995.

Sandes, Karl Olav. "Equality within Patriarchal Structures: Some New
Testament Perspectives on the Christian Fellowship as a Brother-
or Sisterhood and a Family." In *Constructing Early Christian Families: Family as Social Reality and Metaphor*, edited by Halvor
Moxnes, 150–65. New York: Routledge, 1997.

Schaff, Philip, ed. and trans. John Chrysostom's Homily 10 on Second
Timothy (4:9-13). *From Nicene and Post-Nicene Fathers*. Vol. 13. First
Series. Buffalo, NY: Christian Literature Publishing Co., 1889.
Revised and edited for New Advent by Kevin Knight. http://
www.newadvent.org/fathers/230710.htm.

Schottroff, Luise. "Women as Followers of Jesus in New Testament Times." In *The Bible and Liberation: Political and Social Hermeneutics*, edited by Norman K. Gottwald and Richard Horsley, 458–59. Maryknoll, NY: Orbis, 1993.

Soards, Marion. *1 Corinthians*. New International Biblical Commentary. Peabody, MA: Henrickson, 1999.

Soule, Richard M. "Co-Workers: Prisca and Aquila." *Ekklesia: Then and Now* 62 (October 18, 2005): 1–5.

Spencer, F. Scott. *Journeying through Acts: A Literary-Cultural Reading*. Peabody, MA: Hendrickson, 2004.

———. "Women of 'the Cloth' in Acts: Sewing the Word." In *The Feminist Companion to the Acts of the Apostles*, edited by Amy-Jill Levine and Marianne Blickenstaff, 134–54. Cleveland, OH: Pilgrim Press, 2004.

Thurston, Bonnie. *Spiritual Life in the Early Church: The Witness of Acts and Ephesians*. Minneapolis: Augsburg Fortress, 1993.

———. *Women in the New Testament: Questions and Commentary*. New York: Crossroads, 1998.

Trebilco, Paul. "Asia." In *The Book of Acts in Its First-Century Setting*. Vol. 2, *The Book of Acts in Its Graeco-Roman Setting*, edited by David W. J. Gill and Conrad Gempf, 291–362. Grand Rapids, MI: Eerdmans, 1994.

Verner, David. *The Household of God: The Social World of the Pastoral Epistles*. SBL Dissertation Series 71, edited by William Baird. Chico, CA: Scholars Press, 1983.

Walker, William O. "The Portrayal of Aquila and Priscilla in Acts: The Question of Sources." *New Testament Studies* 54, no. 4 (2008): 478–95.

Walker, J., J. Sheppard, and H. Browne, trans., and revised by George B. Stevens. John Chrysostom's Homily 30 on Romans (15:25–16:5). *From Nicene and Post-Nicene Fathers*. Vol. 11. First Series. Edited by Philip Schaff. Buffalo, NY: Christian Literature Publishing Co., 1889. Revised and edited for New Advent by Kevin Knight. http://www.newadvent.org/fathers/210230.htm.

———. John Chrysostom's Homily 40 on the Acts of the Apostles (18:18). *From Nicene and Post-Nicene Fathers*. Vol. 11. First Series. Edited by Philip Schaff. Buffalo, NY: Christian Literature Publishing Co., 1889. Revised and edited for New Advent by Kevin Knight. http://www.newadvent.org/fathers/210140.htm.

Weifel, Wolfgang. "The Jewish Community in Ancient Rome and the Origins of Roman Christianity." In *The Romans Debate*, edited by Karl P. Donfried, 85-101. Rev. and exp. ed. Peabody, MA: Hendrickson, 1991.

Whitehead, James and Evelyn. *Method in Ministry. Theological Reflection and Christian Ministry.* Rev. ed. Franklin, WI: Sheed and Ward, 1999.

Winter, Miriam Therese. *WomanWord: A Feminist Lectionary and Psalter.* New York: Crossroads. 1991.

Witherington III, Ben. *The Acts of the Apostles: A Socio-Rhetorical Commentary.* Grand Rapids, MI: Eerdmans, 1998.

———. "The Anti-Feminist Tendencies of the 'Western' Text in Acts." *Journal of Biblical Literature* 103, no. 1 (1984): 82–84.

———, and Darlene Hyatt. *Paul's Letter to the Romans: A Socio-Rhetorical Commentary.* Grand Rapids, MI: Eerdmans, 2004.

———. *Women in the Earliest Churches.* New York: Cambridge University Press, 1988.

INDEX OF PERSONS AND SUBJECTS

SCRIPTURE AND ANCIENT AUTHORS INDEX